WEALTH AND FAMILIES

LESSONS FROM MY LIFE JOURNEY

HOWARD STEVENSON

with

SHIRLEY SPENCE

Copyright © 2016 by Howard Stevenson

All rights reserved.

No part of this publication may be reproduced, stored in or introduced into a retrieval system; or transmitted, in any form, or by any means (electronic, mechanical, photocopying, recording or otherwise) without the prior permission of the publisher. Requests for permission should be directed to the publisher:

> Timberline LLC
> P.O. Box 639
> Belmont, MA 02478
> Email: wealthandfamilies@gmail.com

Library of Congress information forthcoming.

ISBN: 978-0-9837486-6-3 (paperback)
ISBN: 978-0-9837486-7-0 (hard cover)
ISBN: 978-0-9837486-8-7 (ebook)

Printed in the United States of America.

Dedication

I offer these lessons learned from my life journey, with gratitude to those of you who have shared the ride. Thank you for all I have learned from you, and for the pleasure of your company. I wish you success—however you choose to define it— on your own unique journey.

Have fun!

Howard

CONTENTS

INTRODUCTION	About This Book	1

PART I: MY LIFE, SO FAR — 4

CHAPTER 1	Heritage, Childhood, and Education	5
CHAPTER 2	Career, Family, and Wealth	18
CHAPTER 3	Live and Learn: My Six Truths	33

PART II: BUILDING AND MANAGING WEALTH — 40

CHAPTER 4	Nature and Dynamics of Wealth	41
CHAPTER 5	My Approach to Wealth Management	56
CHAPTER 6	What I Think I Know about Investing	67
CHAPTER 7	Getting and Using Professional Help	76

PART III: WEALTH AND FAMILIES — 88

CHAPTER 8	A Rebuttal to Family Wealth Models	89
CHAPTER 9	My Philosophy of Family Wealth	102
CHAPTER 10	Raising Wealthy Kids	108
CONCLUSION	The Game of Life	119
APPENDIX	Wealth Quotations	122

Acknowledgments	124
Author Biographies	126
Index	128
Praise for *Wealth and Families*	139
Ordering Information	143

INTRODUCTION

WEALTH PROFESSIONALS LIKE to divide rich people into two categories: acquirers and inheritors. This book is for and about both. It essentially is a case study of someone who made and managed his own money—with much help, of course—and has given a lot of thought to the subject of wealth and families.

WHY WEALTH AND FAMILIES?

IF THIS WAS 1963 and you worked for General Motors, you could expect lifetime employment and long-term, subsidized health care. You wouldn't need to worry too much about the future. That's still the assumption of some government employees but for the rest of us, the world is a different place.

There is a lot more uncertainty and a lot less security today and probably well into the future. Jobs and companies come and go, and I wouldn't bet on Social Security or Medicare. The financial world is increasingly complex too, with lots of ups and downs.

The bottom line is that you can't afford *not* to think about wealth: what you'll need, how you'll get it, and how you'll use it.

Many of us have the nice-to-have problem of wealth. And amid the ongoing debate about the polarization of wealth, more people are becoming wealthy. A recent study estimated the number of millionaire households in the U.S. alone at 7.1 million, including 1.1 new millionaires.[1]

In addition, much has been written about an inheritance boom, with some experts predicting the greatest wealth transfer in history.[2] Whether

---

1. *Global Wealth 2014: Riding a Wave of Growth*, Boston Consulting Group, June 9, 2014.
2. *A Golden Age of Philanthropy Still Beckons: National Wealth Transfer and Potential for Philanthropy*, John J. Havens and Paul G. Schervish, Boston College Center on Wealth and Philanthropy, May 28, 2014.

you agree with their numbers or not, the question of how to raise children in the context of wealth keeps many rich parents up at night.

A whole industry has sprung up to help you deal with these issues. But as you will see, I don't agree with a lot of what the so-called experts espouse. Not everyone loves a critic, I know, but my intent is in the spirit of Abraham's Lincoln's words, "He has a right to criticize, who has a heart to help."

ABOUT THIS BOOK

A FEW YEARS AGO, some family members suggested that I share what I have learned during my first 74 years in a book for the family, especially the grandchildren. I was happy to oblige but with a caveat: I don't profess to have all the answers.

Much of what I've learned has been acquired through trial and error. The syllogism is true: "Good decisions come from wisdom, wisdom comes from experience, and experience comes from bad decisions." I have made my share of mistakes, as you will see, but hopefully learned from them.

Capturing what I've learned during my first 74 years involved storytelling and opinionating from me, questions and scribbling by my co-author Shirley Spence, and conversations with family members and others who have influenced my thinking about wealth, investing, families and life in general.

The family book is called *Howard's Journey: Lessons from the Game of Life*. (The game metaphor will return fairly often, in the pages to come.)

Howard's Journey was a labor of love, not intended for a public audience. I have shared it with a few close friends, however, and given a few talks based on its key ideas. The response—"Where can I get a copy?!"—has persuaded me to share parts of it with you in this book.

Wealth and Families is divided into three main parts and a concluding section, with an appendix. Here's how it flows:

- ◆ *Part I—My Life, So Far* is a largely chronological review of my life journey followed by a summary of what I call my six truths.

- ◆ *Part II—Building and Managing Wealth* shares how I think about wealth, discusses my approach to wealth management and investing, and offers some thoughts on getting and using help.

- *Part III—Wealth and Families* presents my somewhat contrarian views on the almost undiscussable topic of wealth and families, and offers some advice for raising wealthy kids.

- *Conclusion—The Game of Life* will cycle back to my life's journey. I'll offer some "tips for winning" and, on a more serious note, share a poem that I find inspiring and hope you will too.

- The *Appendix* will offer some of the many quotes we found about wealth from across centuries, continents and cultures.

Now, who might be interested in reading *Wealth and Families?*

Friends and colleagues who are curious about the family book will find that it covers a large part of the territory in a more digestible format. The broader audience is people who have made their money or who are on their way, and those who advise them. For example:

- People just beginning their wealth journeys may find it interesting to read about mine, and be able to learn something from my thinking and choices and where they took me.

- People who already have achieved some wealth and are trying to manage it may find something of value, whether as individuals or family offices.

- Wealthy parents may appreciate some practical advice and a framework for talking to their kids about wealth.

- Wealth professionals may find it a useful tool for their clients, to help them reflect on wealth and families and perhaps get some ideas for tackling issues that they face.

Not everything that I say will be relevant to each reader, of course. But some people have found my experiences and some of the principles derived from them helpful, either because they are right or because they cause people to formulate their own views as they disagree.

We've tried to make *Wealth and Families* an entertaining read; you'll find family photos, cartoons, quotes and lots of stories. Most of all, we hope that what you read in the coming pages will be of some help to you—or someone you care about—on your own journey.

MY LIFE, SO FAR

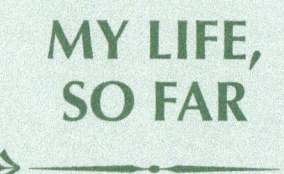

ONE YEAR, WHEN I celebrated another birthday, my friend and colleague Harvard Business School Dean Jay Light sent me an e-mail that said, "Can't possibly believe how old you are tonight!" I echo that sentiment but I am not ungrateful. Dying once, and coming close three times more, will do that for you.

Part I describes my life journey, more or less chronologically. *Chapter 1* describes my heritage, childhood, and education. *Chapter 2* covers career, family, and wealth and closes with some reflections on life. *Chapter 3* shares some rules of the road that I've learned along the way.

Through all that, you will see the evolution of my thinking over the years, much of which has been captured in books that I have written or co-authored. (I often don't know what I'm thinking until I am forced to write it down in a more or less linear and coherent fashion.)

Most importantly, my story offers just one example of someone trying to navigate life, placing bets and learning along the way. It flows from the stories of ancestors who saw and seized opportunities when they arose. Serendipity also comes into play, as you will see.

HERITAGE, CHILDHOOD, AND EDUCATION

PIONEERS AND MORMONS, math, Stanford, and Harvard Business School (HBS). My heritage, childhood, and education built a strong foundation for my life while also expanding my horizons. Let the journey begin!

MY HERITAGE

FAMILY LORE IS an interesting and informative thing. I vividly recall my grandmother telling me a story that, when I did a fact check, couldn't possibly have been true. Oh well, it was a good story. Here's my best effort at an accurate account of my heritage.

Being raised Mormon helps; my parents tried to keep good records. The ancestral charts shown on the next two pages (see **Figures 1-1** and **1-2**) were developed by my father in the 1960s as part of his fascination with genealogy. (There are many more charts.)

Most of my lineage is from the British Isles. I can trace some of my roots as far back as the 1500s. With a leap of faith, there is evidence of one family name in the *Doomsday Book's* census of landholders in England and Wales, conducted in 1086 by William the Conqueror.

Working backward from my parents is a challenge, however.

Stevenson is hard to trace because it is a patrinominal name; somebody in the line was a son of Steven. Higginbotham (my mother's maiden

6 ◆ Wealth & Families

FIGURE 1-1
Ancestral Photo Chart

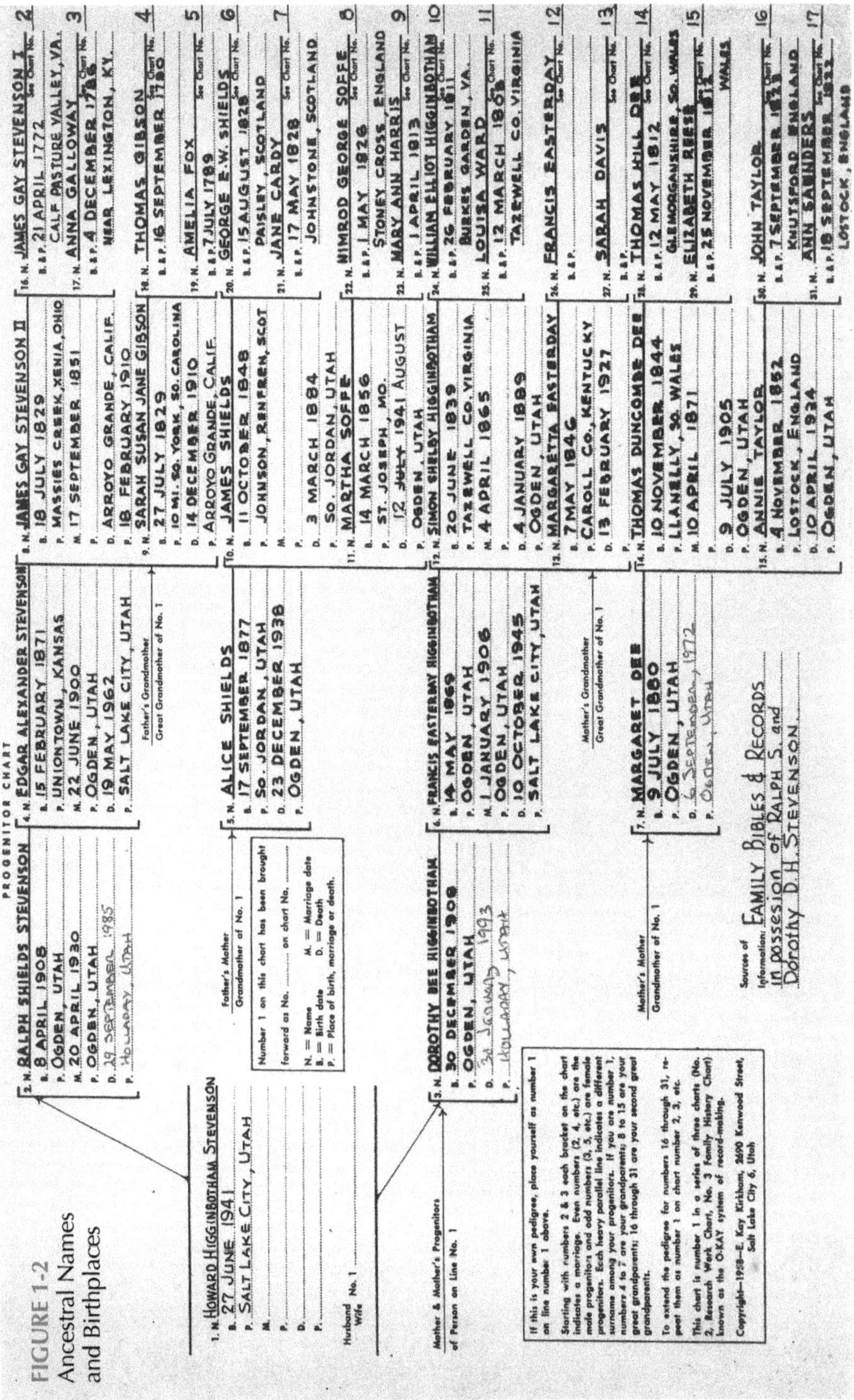

FIGURE 1-2
Ancestral Names and Birthplaces

name) means "down by the oak tree at the river" and came from someone in the chain being a foundling, according to family lore.[3]

If you look back six or seven generations, people were born, lived and died within a ten-mile radius. Then, almost everyone moved. Each story is unique but they all demonstrate great courage. The lesson I take from them is: Don't be afraid of change and taking risks.

Much of the immigration from Europe was in the early 1700s, except for the Mormon side where it occurred in the mid-1800s. Some parts of all the families share the distinction of being Sons and Daughters of the American Revolution.

I was taught that we were part of the mid-nineteenth-century pioneer movement.[4] All of my great-grandparents moved west before the railroad was finished in 1869. They were tough characters, as illustrated by these two stories:

- My great-grandfather Higginbotham was raised in the Blue Ridge Mountains, and got married five days before the Treaty of Appomattox. He and his bride promptly left war-ravaged Virginia for Ogden, Utah.

- My great-grandmother Dee chronicled her story in a book called *Memoirs of a Handcart Pioneer*. In it, she describes how her family pushed its possessions in a handcart all the way from St. Joseph, Missouri, to Ogden.

Great-grandfather Dee founded several companies, one of which was sold to General Electric 60 years after his death. His son-in-law (my grandfather Higginbotham) was less astute about business but managed to raise his family, including my mother, in relative privilege.

The Stevenson side was of more modest means. Grandfather Stevenson was born in a sod house in Kansas in 1872, and lured further west by the Colorado Silver Rush. His relatives settled in California, but he headed to Ogden to teach at a school for the deaf and blind, and later serve as assistant postmaster.

---

3. It also is said that the Easterday line may be a foundling story (i.e., someone found somewhere on Easter Day).

4. "Come, Come, Ye Saints," a hymn we often sang, captured that pioneer spirit. (See https://www.youtube.com/watch?v=4ia3gYSvG8M for a rendition by the Mormon Tabernacle Choir.)

My parents, Ralph Stevenson and Dorothy Higginbotham, both were born and raised in Ogden. They began dating in high school. My father was interested in technology and radio and went on to technical school in Chicago, a 1,100-mile train ride away.

Jobs were scarce in Ogden, but my father found one in Chicago. Worried that my mother would find another suitor, however, he quit and came home to Ogden. My parents were 22 and 21 years old when they married in 1930, just as the Depression was starting.

The newlyweds moved in with my Higginbotham grandparents in Salt Lake City. My father got a job working the night shift at KSL, the Mormon radio station. He also enrolled as an officer in the Naval reserve.

My mother was a proper lady, which meant she never had a paying job. However, she was reputed to be the first female ham radio operator in Utah. Until she died, she could read code at 20 words per minute, and send it even faster.

My brother was born in Salt Lake City on May 11, 1935. I came along about six years later, on June 27, 1941. I usually say that I was raised in Holladay, Utah but we didn't actually settle there until I was nine years old; World War II intervened.

Me in a good mood

MY CHILDHOOD YEARS

MY FATHER WAS activated to Hawaii in April 1941, a few months before my birth. My mother, brother and I joined him there in September 1941, moving into housing some distance from the naval base at Pearl Harbor. On December 7, the Japanese bombs fell.

My father, fortunately, was on a small ship moored outside of Battleship Row, and made it safely out of the harbor. He was redeployed to the South Pacific to lead a joint Army–Navy radio installation team, and then sent to the Aleutian Islands. He never discussed the war, but he was in many nasty battles.

My mother, brother and I were evacuated from Hawaii in April 1942. We went back to Salt Lake City and then moved in with an aunt and uncle in Ohio. When my father returned to the States, we joined him briefly in San Francisco, and followed him to his next posting in Washington, D.C.

At the end of the war, we moved back to Salt Lake City, sharing a two-bedroom duplex with my grandparents. (We lived in side-by-side units.) When my grandfather died, my grandmother was left not wealthy but comfortable enough.

On September 25, 1947, my sister was born. It was getting a little cramped; it was time to move on. My parents bought a two-and-a-half-acre piece of land in Holladay, Utah, just ten miles from Salt Lake City. It was a beautiful area, surrounded by farmlands with views of Mount Olympus in the distance.

My parents built a Y-shaped house with separate wings for my grandmother Higginbotham and our family, and some common areas. It was a nice home, nicer than we could afford really, and possible only because my father did a lot of the work on it himself. (He let my brother and me "help.")

Back in the civilian work force, my father built on his Navy communication skills, taking a job in a radio supply store. Next, he opened a business installing custom sound systems. When that failed, he became a manufacturer's sales representative, selling products for a variety of electronics manufacturers.

Dad worked hard and was on the road a lot, covering a huge swath of territory. He didn't make a lot of money but he was appreciated wherever he went. He lived two values that have stuck with me: "Offer help to anyone who asks for it" and "Deliver more value than you're paid for."

My parents were very supportive. They were proud of their family. I still have a huge scrapbook with clippings of my various lifetime accomplishments, which they put together in their later years. (They did the same for my brother and sister.)

I do recall my mother eagerly (sometimes anxiously) awaiting the arrival of my father's sales commission checks, but she didn't complain. Her motto was: "Success is getting what you want; happiness is wanting what you get." (My corollary is: "Marry a happy person.")

Grandmother Higginbotham was a financial safety net of sorts for our family. I surmise that she made more than a few mortgage payments for

Me in my first car

my parents. The niceties were provided by her too. She paid for Boy Scout camps and helped me buy my first car.

I never felt deprived growing up, but lots of things weren't possible and there was a sense of financial insecurity that stuck with me over many years. As an adult, I never wanted to have to worry about paying the bills, and I didn't want to cause anxiety about money to my family.

My father's sister (Aunt Zola) and her husband (Uncle Boyd) moved from Ohio to split the Holladay plot with us, building their home next door to ours. My grandfather Stevenson moved in with them, some years after his second wife died.

Aunt Zola and Uncle Boyd had no children of their own and were like a second set of parents to me. They ran a lawnmower sales and repair business called Boyd Martin Company. My aunt was a professional accountant and handled the books.

When I was a teenager, I started working for them as a sales associate and delivery boy every Saturday and summers, for seventy cents an hour. I learned some accounting, some mechanics and a lot of salesmanship. I also got a lesson in respect for working people.

My mother's privileged past would show sometimes, I must admit; she'd say things like "our kind of people." When I showed some "attitude" one day with a mechanic, my uncle said, "Can you do his work? Until you are as productive as him, shut up." I got it.

Uncle Boyd and my father were almost the complete opposites in temperament. My father was a perfectionist; "Do it right" was his motto. My uncle said, "Just do it." He encouraged experimentation, and always had interesting books around. (I was an avid reader.)

I credit my appreciation for the environment to my grandfather Stevenson, an active outdoorsman. When he retired, he and his second wife drove all through the western states, towing a trailer. (I have his scrapbooks of nature photos from those trips.) He was climbing mountains until he was 85.

The Mormon Church also was a big part of my younger years; it was the hub of the Holladay community. By my late teens, however, I was questioning many of the Church's stories though not its tenets. My parents accepted that, but some community members were dismayed.

I haven't considered myself a practicing Mormon since then, but the Church's values of family, community, and continuous learning have stuck with me. I also think that my views on personal accountability were shaped by the Church. (More on that later.)

Most people from Holladay don't stray far. Many of my childhood friends live close to where they grew up, married to their high school sweethearts. I was desperate to get to the outside world. My strategy was to get good grades, participate in every contest and activity available, and travel anywhere I could.

My academic grades were straight "A's" although I tended to score lower on citizenship, which was a pseudonym for good behavior. I wasn't bad, and my teachers liked me; I was just—uhm—very *active*. One of my jokes: "If Ritalin had existed when I was growing up, I would have been much less successful."

I joined the Boy Scouts at age 12, and earned enough merit badges to become an Eagle Scout by age 13. I wasn't an athlete but participated in pretty much everything else: Key Club, Junior Achievement, science fairs, state math contests, Model UN contests, chess club, stage club . . . and more.

When I was sixteen, I was selected to go to France on the first six-month American Field Service (AFS) school program for Americans abroad.

My host family was quite affluent, and lived across the street from the Palace of Versailles. They spoke no English and I didn't speak French so it was tricky, at home and at school, but I was exposed to art and other things that I'd never seen before.

My relationships with my siblings reflected our big age differences. (It was like raising three only children, for my parents.) We led more or less separate lives. I stayed in touch with them though, and remained close with my parents over the years.

Looking back on all that, I realize how strongly I was shaped by the community in which I was raised and the experiences that it afforded me.

There was tremendous influence not just from my parents but also from my uncle and aunt, grandparents, and the extended family that you met at family reunions. Some inspired me. Others made me see the importance of an exit path, for me.

My teachers also inspired me, especially my math teacher, George Barton. (I still sponsor a scholarship in his name at Olympus High School in Holladay.) I attribute my "live life forward" philosophy partly to another of my high school teachers, Miss Little, who had us read a poem called "Miniver Cheevy."[5]

I go back to Holladay from time to time, for family events and high school reunions. In 2013, I was inducted into the Olympus Alumni Hall of Fame, along with a woman who also strayed from the traditional Holladay path. (She became the Episcopal Church Bishop of Utah.)

HIGHER (AND HIGHER) EDUCATION

WHEN THE TIME came for me to apply to colleges, I was still in France. I was a finalist in the National Merit program, so there would be some scholarship money. Where to apply? (There weren't a lot of heavy analytics involved in the decision making, as you will see.)

I had visited Yale on my way to France; I applied there. I had heard of Stanford because Jack Curtis, the football coach at the University of Utah, had gone there; I applied there too. The University of Utah was my back up plan. What about Harvard, you ask? I had never heard of it.

I think I was admitted to Yale or at least a scholarship amount was discussed, and I know I was accepted to Stanford. The Stanford scholarship was slightly better than Yale's, and I figured I could get rides home from California with friends for Christmas. Decision made!

Stanford was an eye-opener for me in many ways. For one, it was my first encounter with different models of success. Also, I had been exposed

---

5. If you're interested, you can find the poem at *http://www.poemtree.com/poems/Miniver Cheevy.htm*.

to different kinds of wealth growing up, but Stanford was at a whole different level.

I met the son of the Paper Mate Products founder who sold his business to Gillette, the grandson of Union Bank of California's founder, the grandson of Dow Chemical's founder, and the son of the head of a steel services mega-chain. They went to Tahiti for winter break; I hoped I could it make it home to Utah.

My freshman summer, I wanted to work at a national park, but decided to work for my aunt and uncle again and live at home, to save money. I could make $50 a week, which came to $700 for the summer, and would make a nice dent in my college bill. (Tuition, room and board were $1,450 per year.)

I pretty much kept my head down at Stanford, and studied. I also managed an eating club in exchange for food and $100 per month, and was very involved in creating the student union. My best friends were the five guys I roomed with for most of the final three years, all Phi Beta Kappa's.

My second year of college, I attended a six-month program at a small Stanford campus just outside of Stuttgart, Germany in the metropolis of Beutelsbach bei Stuttgart. I'm not sure that I got what Stanford was trying to give us, but it was a wonderful experience.

We lived in a dorm, had classes in a rather sparse building, and were exposed to a lot of post-WWII Europe. Stuttgart and Berlin still had bomb damage. The Berlin Wall hadn't been built. The Deutsch mark was 4.14 to the dollar, and you could stay in a reasonable country hotel for $2.

Back on the academic front, picking a major at Stanford wasn't too hard. I was a math geek (and still am). I was fascinated with the new world of computers, huge banks of them with less computing power than a modern laptop.

I crossed math off my career list though, as I realized that others were better at it and there were relatively few academic jobs in the field. (I must make a brief aside here to mention that while I opted not to become a math professional, math has strongly influenced how I view and navigate the world.)[6]

I considered software engineering as a career for a while. It built on my math skills and was a growing field. I tried it out the summers before

---

6. If the subject interests you, I recommend a book called *How Not to Be Wrong: The Power of Mathematical Thinking*, Jordan Ellenberg, The Penguin Press, 2014.

and after my senior year by working at IBM. I crossed that off my list too, however; I lacked a real passion for it, and preferred a more people-oriented activity.

It surprises most people, but a military career was a serious option for me. I admired my father's Navy service; he was promoted to commander before the war ended. My brother was one of the youngest captains in the Marine Corps.

I figured I could be a good strategist or a logistics expert but I knew that I didn't have a military leadership kind of personality. I'm a bit of an introvert (that surprises people too) and an intellectual free spirit (that doesn't).

My Stanford photo

I graduated from Stanford in 1963, with distinction in mathematics. I didn't attend my graduation ceremony because it was ten days after dorm housing ended, so it would have cost money to stay somewhere. My family wasn't planning to come out anyway, although they were very proud.

Aunt Zola and Uncle Boyd had asked me to take over their business after graduation so they could retire. It was hard but I said "no." It wasn't that I didn't care about them or that a business career didn't interest me. I just wanted something bigger than Holladay. (They sold the business, and retired.)

Business school seemed a good experiment, to see if business was a deep interest and whether I had what it took to succeed. Also, an MBA wouldn't preclude any of my nonbusiness interests and might open up some new options. (I did consider law school but didn't pursue it because it took three years.)

I was accepted into the Stanford and HBS MBA programs. I chose HBS in part because it offered a larger stipend. Off I went to Boston, an eager member of the Class of 1965. HBS proved to be another eye opener. I loved the case method.

You develop great analytical skills working through what seemed like 1,000 cases, six days a week. It was only years later, though, that I realized you also develop an entrepreneurial attitude. There's no "right answer" to a case; you have to solve the problem at hand even if you lack resources, information or power. And in every situation, there is an opportunity.

I had the great fortune, at HBS, to be taken under the wing of Professor Myles Mace, a corporate management guru. Our many conversations turned out to be the first major inflection point in my professional life.[7]

Professor Mace helped me understand that I had a passion for business and business education, and might have a competitive advantage in the field.

It hit me when he was talking about his own career path, explaining that he essentially had based it on asking three questions: "Where did you get that number? What does it mean? Why are you trying to bullshit me?"

I got it. I understood the power of the simple act of asking the right questions. Then, he helped me to see that I was really good at figuring out the key strategic questions to ask in business situations; that became the cornerstone for my life's work.

I wasn't entirely sure what I would do after graduation.

Consulting appealed to my analytical side. Investment banking looked more interesting after I saw the film "The Wheeler Dealers." I still remember one of James Garner's lines, as a Texas oil tycoon who goes to New York City to play in the stock market: "I just stand in the flow, and try to take a piece." Not a bad definition of investment banking!

Then, there was the professor option. It paid less—$9,000 versus an investment banker's $12,000—but you didn't have to dress up in expensive clothes.

I applied for and was accepted into the HBS Doctoral Program, with a Ford Foundation Fellowship. I decided to stay at HBS and see what happened. (It didn't hurt that the draft board in Holladay was proud of me, and gave me a 2-S deferment just as the war in Vietnam heated up.)

In June 1965, I picked up my MBA diploma, and got married. (I met my future wife during my second year at HBS.) I began my doctoral studies and research for a dissertation called "Defining Corporate Strengths and Weaknesses." I also took on a job as a research assistant and instructor in Business Policy.

Money was tight but my wife and I got by, first on my $300 monthly doctoral stipend and then the $500-per-month from the first HBS job. We

---

7. By inflection point, I mean a pivotal event in your life, whether positive or negative. How you respond is as important as the event itself.

bought a used VW for $1,100, and went from a $90-per-month student apartment in Cambridge to a $175-per-month apartment in Arlington.

When my grandmother gave each of her grandchildren $20,000, I felt quite rich. I used part of it to pay for tuition at Boston University, where my wife was pursuing a bachelor's degree, and put the rest in the bank for future expenses. It felt good to have a cushion.

I finished my dissertation in three years and a month. The logical next step: a faculty position and the start of a long career described in *Chapter 2*.

I can't leave this chapter, however, without reiterating the importance of both Stanford and HBS in my personal and professional development.

I was a grateful scholarship student at both schools, and I am proud to be able to give back as an alumnus. I regularly attend Stanford reunions and have built a long and deep relationship with Harvard. I cherish the many friendships and professional relationships made on both campuses, over many years.

Now, on to the next chapter of my journey—career, family, and wealth.

CAREER, FAMILY, AND WEALTH

TEACHING AND LEARNING, investing and philanthropy, family and more family, more wealth than I ever imagined. The story of my journey continues, followed by some reflections on life from a grateful 74-year-old.

MY 20'S AND 30'S

IN 1968, AT 27 years old, I started my career at HBS as an Assistant Professor in Business Policy. My wife and I were able to sublet a two-bedroom faculty apartment in Cambridge, which was a real coup because normally you could only get a one-bedroom if you didn't have children.

In 1969, I bought a house in Lexington for $39,000. You could call it a "handyman's special," a rundown house in a nice area. It was the first of a long—and quite lucrative—string of projects where I would buy a place, move in, fix it up, and move on. (That Lexington house is now worth $400,000.)

My parents were getting on in years by then and having health challenges. I wanted to help financially so I borrowed $300,000 from them, invested it, and paid it all back with 6% interest. I figured I had better earning potential and could take the risk. It was painful, but it gave them regular income. I also took out life insurance on myself, so they wouldn't worry.

By 1970, I had been teaching two years and had become a father. (Our first son was born that January.)

I was 29 years old, earning $15,000 as a professor. I wasn't excited about doing consulting on the side like my colleagues were doing, even though they were getting paid quite handsomely by places like GE. It wasn't interesting to me plus it didn't feel like my skill set.

In 1970, Matt Simmons approached me about joining the small investment bank/advisory firm that he had founded in Boston. I knew Matt from HBS, and I was interested in learning more about investing. Matt's salary offer wasn't bad either.

I requested and was granted a two-year leave of absence from HBS, and joined Simmons Associates in 1970 as a vice president. I didn't know where that would lead, but I must admit to having largely decided that I would not be returning to HBS.

Will and me, the new dad

Meanwhile, on the home front, our family grew with the arrival of our second son in 1972. I bought another fixer-upper house in Lincoln. My total net worth—four years out of HBS —was approximately $100,000.

I was enjoying working with Matt, but the early 1970s brought some tough economic times. Looking ahead, I didn't see a lot of opportunity with Simmons. I began exploring other options.

I was interviewing on Wall Street when Boston Safe Deposit and Trust, one of our clients at Simmons, offered me a position as vice president of finance in its real estate investment trust (REIT) business, which appealed to my interest in real estate because of the inherent possibility of leverage.

I was close to accepting the offer, and went to HBS to say that I wasn't coming back. Strangely (I thought), they asked if I would be interested in teaching a real estate course. I believed that there would be no better way to learn about real estate than to teach it.

Back to HBS I went, as Lecturer in Real Property Asset Management. I started a course in 1972 that proved quite popular, and began recruiting faculty. I went across the river to Harvard's Graduate School of Design to woo Bill Poorvu, a real estate developer who also taught Urban Planning.

Bill came on as Lecturer, then Adjunct Professor (the first and only person with that title). Together we wrote over sixty cases, and developed a framework for studying real estate management with four elements: people, property, deal and environment.[8] Our friendship became one of the turning points in my life.

I also invested in 125 South End apartments with Peter Wilde and several others. There were many sleepless nights when interest rates jumped. Real estate was risky and too time-intensive for me, I realized. It requires a lot of hands-on attention to tend to properties and their occupants.

About this time, I started joining boards. My strategy was to go for smaller companies and get a piece of the action. Realty Income Trust and Wolfe Industries were my first forays, in 1973. A few dozen more directorships would follow over the years. Each one was a new learning opportunity, which I loved.

Realty Income Trust introduced me to Royal Little, the founder of Textron, and to Rob Freeman, who became a wonderful friend. Connecticut General's REIT taught me not to trust investment banks. Scientific Systems Services taught me the problems of a public company. Preco, a Simmons client that invited me to join its board, exposed me to the challenges of a small, privately held company.

Cut to 1974.

I was 33 years old with three kids. (My third son came along in 1974.) I was on my third home project, one of the most inappropriate houses in one of the best spots in Lincoln. (I sold the first Lincoln home at a tidy profit.)

I also had taken on my first nonprofit board role, as a trustee of Lincoln's Rural Land Foundation (RLF). I didn't have any money to give but I donated a portion of my property, and they valued my real estate expertise and deal-making skills. (They are still getting cash flow from one deal that I helped structure.)

At HBS, I was having a ball teaching real estate, and earned tenure in 1977. But that came with the Dean's suggestion that I "do something important," which I took as a signal that real estate was not a highly valued subject area at HBS. Not a good sign, for an academic career.

Also, I had interviewed some senior faculty members, and discovered that most were not happy.

---

8. That framework would morph into People, Context, Deal and Opportunity, when it was adapted for use in the entrepreneurship area by Bill Sahlman.

They had chased and won the prize but felt trapped. They were very good at what they did, but they didn't see a way to change direction, even if they were bored. I call that the velvet-lined rut; it can happen in any career.

I asked myself, "Is this what I really want?" I wasn't sure. I decided to get some hands-on management experience. In 1978, I accepted a position as CFO of Preco, a $100+-million paper company with 1,200 employees, based in West Springfield, MA. I moved the family to nearby Suffield, CT.

Preco was a challenge. Telephone calls were still routed through operators with obsolete plug boards, a nonperformance suit against a contractor hired to modernize plant operations dragged on for years, oil prices soared, the economy tanked, and bankruptcy loomed.

But it taught me about real business—unions, creditors and all—and set the stage for my interest in implementation as well as strategy. It also allowed me to be home most evenings, and have time for family and personal interests.

MY 40'S

AFTER THREE YEARS, I felt that I had learned all I could at Preco. My net worth now at $1 million, I set myself a new goal of $5 million. (My thinking was that at 6%, I could take out $300,000 annually for living expenses, if necessary. That seems highly optimistic now.)

I was considering Wall Street or venture capital as my next career move. Then I got an unexpected visit from the new HBS Dean, John McArthur. (John and I had become friends as young faculty colleagues.) He had a problem.

HBS had been struggling with entrepreneurship for decades.[9] Despite some sporadic advances, it had no clear track record for academic achievement. The problem had taken on a new urgency for John. The latest MBA catalogue listed a course called Starting New Ventures, but no one on the permanent HBS faculty wanted to teach it.

Students were in the Dean's office, demanding to know why it wasn't being offered. John needed someone not just to teach the course, but also

---

9. This story is documented in *Shaping the Waves: A History of Entrepreneurship at Harvard Business School* by Jeff Cruikshank, Harvard Business Review Press, 2005.

to take on the job of building the intellectual and organizational foundation for entrepreneurship at HBS.

John had decided that "someone" was me and made his pitch: "If you come back, I'll back you with all I have."

I thought that sounded like fun, and I had faith in John. Back to HBS I went in 1982, without a really clear idea of what I was going to do. I was honored to be named the first Sarofim–Rock Professor of Business Administration.

The chair was important as a testament to HBS' long-term commitment to entrepreneurship. It had been generously endowed by two MBA'51 classmates: the legendary Silicon Valley pioneer Arthur Rock, and Fayez Sarofim, a famous Houston money manager.

Among HBS faculty, however, there still was a good deal of skepticism about entrepreneurship. We needed to get credible research talent as well as great teachers, and integrate entrepreneurship with other disciplines. I decided to start with a colloquium on entrepreneurship for the HBS community.

Drawing on my experiences in real estate—where your typical firm takes other people's resources and assembles them—I came up with the definition of entrepreneurship as "the pursuit of opportunity beyond the resources currently controlled." (That definition seems to be holding up over time.)

Our credibility was helped by an External Relations survey conducted by Paula Duffy. It showed that nearly a third of HBS alumni were self-employed in 1983, and almost half described themselves as entrepreneurs. That got some faculty attention.

I was able to lure Bill Sahlman over from Finance, John Kao from Organizational Behavior, and eventually many other great friends, scholars and teachers. When we gathered enough faculty members, the entrepreneurship group (including real estate) became a faculty unit, and I became its chair.

The faculty grew from four people in 1985 to 35 in 2011, when I retired. We wrote over 1,000 cases and numerous books. Entrepreneurial management now is a required first-year course with numerous second-year electives at HBS, and is taught at many other schools. We also pioneered the concept of social enterprise, now a vibrant field at HBS and elsewhere.

It was an exciting time in the evolution of my thinking as well, especially about change and predictability. In 1987, *Chaos: Making a*

New Science by James Gleick was causing a stir. It reinforced my belief (and observations) that we live in a world of rapid and discontinuous change.

I saw that management theory, which presumed equilibrium to be the norm, was not helpful to managers trying to get from a current state to a desired future state. That led to an article published in 1990 that is still one of my favorites, "Entrepreneurial Management's Need for a More 'Chaotic' Theory."[10]

The dilemma then: how to take action in a seemingly unpredictable world?

As I studied entrepreneurs, I saw some succeed and others fail based on their ability to understand the consequences of an action and then convince other people to see it the same way. There were no guarantees, but you could project ahead and try to get there. *That* was the essence of predicting.

In 1995, Mihnea Moldoveanu and I published a *Harvard Business Review* article called "The Power of Predictability," which discussed the organizational and managerial implications. My fascination with predictability in business and life continued over the years, yielding more than one book on it.[11]

As I studied venture capital, my views on predictability began to leech into my thinking about investing. Nobody was very good at it, so what was the best strategy? A lot had to do with being able to distinguish a good decision from a bad decision, I concluded, and accepting that there was no guaranteed outcome.

Meanwhile, thanks to Bill Poorvu, a huge personal opportunity was building: Baupost, a now legendary hedge fund with $29 billion assets under management.

In 1982, I became one of Baupost's four co-founders and its first president. (Its name was conceived on a beach in the Caribbean, where Bill combined letters of the founders' names: <u>Ba</u>ruch, <u>Au</u>erbach, <u>Po</u>orvu and <u>St</u>evenson.)

---

10. "Entrepreneurial Management's Need for a More 'Chaotic' Theory," Howard Stevenson, Susan Harmeling, *Journal of Business Venturing*, Vol. 5, No. 1, January 1990.

11. *Do Lunch or Be Lunch: The Power of Predictability in Creating Your Future*, Howard H. Stevenson with Jeffrey L. Cruikshank, Harvard Business School Press, 1998. *Make Your Own Luck: 12 Practical Steps to Taking Smarter Risks in Business*, Eileen C. Shapiro and Howard H. Stevenson, Penguin Group, 2005.

Baupost co-founders

It made for busy times all through the 1980s, hustling back and forth between the HBS campus and the Baupost office in Harvard Square almost every day.

On the home front, I moved the family to Southborough when I returned to HBS. It was a deliberate alternative to a rich town like Lincoln. (I didn't want my young sons growing up to believe that they were entitled to a Porsche in high school.) Southborough public schools were fine, and I could hop on the Mass Pike to get to work.

I bought seven acres and built a pretty big house. I couldn't really afford it, so there was a lot of structure and not much finish. My fixer-upper skills again were put to use, with "help" from the boys. (Always smart to put the young ones to work hammering nails that no one will see, I find.)

In 1985, I bought my first vacation home, a ski condo at Okemo Mountain in Vermont, and learned to ski. (There hadn't been money for skiing growing up in Utah.) It proved popular with family and friends, and I bought a second condo there in 1987 for overflow guests.

I was building up paper wealth thanks to my prospective performance fees from Baupost, but I was highly leveraged. (I got a $30,000 salary and a five-year performance fee.) The problem was that performance fees were paid out at the end of the five years, but income was recognized as you went along, so I was borrowing from the bank to pay taxes on fees that I had yet to see.

June of 1990 brought a major inflection point in my personal life; my wife left. It was a shock, to put it mildly. The boys decided to stay with me, somewhat to my surprise. I was now an almost-49-year-old, single parent of three boys ranging in age from 15 to 20.

I knew that I had to focus my time on managing life; I couldn't handle HBS, Baupost and the family. Seth Klarman, who was 26 when he joined Baupost at its inception in 1982, had grown into a great money manager so I felt comfortable leaving active management of Baupost in December 1990.

I had witnessed divorced friends go through some pretty awful and often lengthy financial squabbles with their exes. I wanted to avoid that.

As it turns out, divorce is a great tax planning opportunity. I took money out of the Baupost performance fee and set up trusts for my ex-wife (in lieu of alimony), and one for my mother-in-law (whom I had been supporting). I also used some of the money to set up a trust for my sons.

After taxes and the transfers to the trusts, my net worth was $5 million in 1991.

With no more Baupost performance fees in my future, I decided that I needed to increase my safety net to $10 million. I metered money into personal investments, figuring I could risk one year's income and always keeping two to three years' income in reserve. My Harvard pension was a nice safety net.

Community-wise, my interest and involvement in land conservation continued. I joined the Sudbury Valley Trustees (SVT), whose work spans 36 towns, as a director in 1991. (I would later serve as president, and then chair of the President's Council.) I also joined the board of the Boston Ballet.

MY 50'S

MY YOUNGEST SON and I were muddling along as two single guys. (The two older boys were at college.) "Making dinner" involved ordering subs from D'Angelo's on most nights. Then I had the good fortune to be introduced to my wife of now 24 years, Fredi.

We were married in January 1992, and Fredi moved to our Southborough home. The Stevenson clan expanded to include her four daughters as well as a grandson who was born to one daughter three weeks before the wedding.

Blending two families with adult children is an interesting experience, especially when they have different styles. In our case, I think there is a healthy respect for our differences as well as our common ground . . . and all with a good sense of humor.

I wanted everyone to feel a sense of financial security, starting with Fredi. She had been through some tough financial times, supporting her family after a difficult divorce. It was important to me that she felt financially independent, so I had a postnuptial agreement drawn up giving her a private fund.

She resisted at first, saying that it wasn't necessary and didn't feel right; that it would signify a lack of trust on her part. But it was as much for me as for her; I didn't want to know when and how she spent her money. We went ahead with it, and it has worked out well all around.

I also wanted to make it clear that Fredi's children would be treated as equals to mine; no second class citizens. I gave each of the girls a sum of money that roughly equaled what each of the boys had in assets at that point. I also offered to pay for graduate school if they wanted. (Three of them did.)

A large family keeps you very busy. We have celebrated graduations, new jobs and careers, weddings, and births and have made our way through some less happy events (including the death of Fredi's and my remaining parents).

My personal investing was a nights-and-weekend project but going quite well; money was accumulating. In 1993, I decided to use $3 million to set up the Stevenson Family Investment Limited Partnership (SFILP). I also set up a charitable trust with $500,000.

At HBS, I continued to chair the entrepreneurship unit until 1998, when I decided that it was time for the younger people to take charge.

Along the way, I did a three-year stint as Senior Associate Dean, Director of Finance and Administration. I also served as faculty chair of the Presidents' Seminar, which was our Young Presidents' Organization program. (It became the most popular program in the YPO system.)

From 1998 through 2000, I focused on executive education, serving as faculty chair of the Owner/President Management program. I began to sense a plot on the part of the Dean to get me out of town, however, when I was named faculty chair of the Latin America Faculty Advisory Group in 1998.

MY 60'S

IN 2001, I hit 60. I was still very active but realized that potentially I was mortal. (The entrepreneur often says, "If I die . . . ." rather than "When I die . . . .")

I began to reflect on what success meant to me, joining forces with Laura Nash on a project that culminated in *Just Enough: Tools for Creating Success in Your Work and Life*.[12] The book seems to help people frame the contradictions that they face in their lives.

In the middle of the Latin America exercise and the *Just Enough* project, along came a new HBS job offer: Senior Associate Dean, Director of External Relations.

I figured external relations would be interesting and easy—give some speeches and talk to people I enjoyed. Then, the Dean threw me a curve ball: "Yes, Howard, but I also want you to run a capital campaign." I wasn't altogether sure what that meant but I signed up.

My external relations role lasted four years. (It turned out to include "road warrior," with over 1,000 personal visits.) The capital campaign had a happy ending. We raised $600 million, about 20% above our target. It was a great experience, working with wonderful people both inside and outside of HBS.

HBS Capital Campaign road warrior (with benefactor HansJoerg Wyss and then Dean Jay Light)

Our success attracted the attention of the folks across the river. I spent the next two years helping with Harvard University's fundraising efforts as Senior Associate Provost and then Vice Provost for Planning and

---

12. *Just Enough: Tools for Creating Success in Your Work and Life*, Laura Nash and Howard Stevenson, John Wiley & Sons, 2004.

Resources. I also took on a directorship at the Harvard Business School Publishing Company.

In 2006, I came back to HBS full-time, to serve as Senior Associate Dean, Director of Publishing and Chair of its Board. Over the next five years, we implemented a new economic model for the publishing business. I also hit retirement age in 2006, and—as they do at HBS—retired and then was hired back as a Baker Foundation Professor.

Meanwhile, SFILP was thriving, requiring increasing amounts of my attention. My two local sons had joined me as general partners (GPs) in 2003 but by 2008, the partnership needed full-time attention. My youngest son (Andy) agreed to take on that role, with the other GPs' help as needed.

At HBS, there would be one more teaching gig. I inherited an MBA elective called Building a Business in the Context of a Life (BBCL) from Myra Hart.

Of course, I felt compelled to revamp the course. Shirley Spence joined me as a research associate. We drew heavily on *Just Enough* frameworks, and challenged students to develop a life plan complete with financial scenarios using a personal financial planning tool that we developed.

There was a glitch, though, as we prepared for BBCL's spring 2007 debut. On January 3, 2007, I was walking across campus after lunch when—as my friend Eric Sinoway describes it—my ticker simply stopped ticking.

It was a shock to everyone including my doctor who, at my annual checkup, had declared me as fit as a fiddle. I was extremely lucky that a number of people jumped in to save my life. The head of HBS Operations, Andy O'Brien, who had just been CPR certified, was nearby. At the HBS Health Service clinic—just steps away—Dr. Bruce Biller used a recently donated defibrillator.

After a 45-minute life-and-death struggle, I was in an ambulance on my way to Mt Auburn Hospital, alive.

I was recuperating until fall but did recover fully. A year later, I had a pacemaker/defibrillator device implanted that literally has saved my life three times. I am very grateful for the equipment and skills that have given me at least nine bonus years.

My heart attack was the first of a string of January family health crises that caused a friend to quip, "The Stevensons should eliminate the month of January from their calendar." Still, life rolled along, including a move to Cambridge and the construction or remodeling of ski houses in Maine and houses in the seaside community of Nonquitt, Massachusetts.

MY 70'S

IN 2011, AT age 70, I formally and finally really retired from HBS. The party thrown by HBS was a truly special event.

A video montage featured some of the many people who helped make my HBS career successful and fun. (Some very good friendships were forged there, too.) Another highlight was the announcement of a chair in my honor. I was proud to introduce Tom Eisenmann as the first incumbent.

Research, I recently learned from a Harvard seminar, says that there are four keys to a successful retirement: (1) make a new cohort to replace your work buddies, (2) keep learning, (3) do something creative, and (4) do something for others.

I think that I am accomplishing those goals. I also have discovered that retirement mainly means that you don't get a paycheck. Happily, that has become irrelevant.

I like to keep busy and I have a hard time saying "no," so retirement hasn't slowed me down all that much. (I tell Fredi that I would rather wear out than rust out.) I do think twice about getting on a plane for a meeting but still sometimes find myself asking, "Why am I doing this?"

I remain co-chair with Bill Poorvu of Baupost's advisory board. I get requests for advice and talks about entrepreneurship. Networking was something I learned rather late in life—I initially thought I was bothering people—but now I enjoy helping people with common interests to connect. I keep my hand in the world of investing, working with my son.

Philanthropy has become a main focus of my time.

I continue to work with HBS and Harvard on major gifts. I am especially proud of the Wyss Institute for Biologically Inspired Engineering, made possible by a $125-million gift from HansJoerg Wyss in 2009. A second gift of $125 million in 2013 has helped to advance its pioneering work.

I also am proud of my nonprofit board work, which has included serving as chair of NPR's board in Washington. These days, Olin College of Engineering, Mount Auburn Hospital, CareGroup, WBUR, Isabella Stewart Gardner Museum, Boston Museum of Science, Smithsonian Astrophysics Observatory, Focused Ultrasound Foundation, and SVT keep me busy.

In 2007, Shirley and I began trying to capture what I have learned from my philanthropic experience. *Getting to Giving: Fundraising the Entrepreneurial Way*[13] was published in 2011, my first foray into self-publishing.

Since then, there have been a lot of talks, seminars and articles and we publish a regular e-newsletter. (Yes, I blog; check out *www.gettingto giving-fundraising.com*.) I really have enjoyed helping people to think differently about fundraising, and to be able to better serve their causes.

Another book was bubbling along in parallel. In 2012, Eric Sinoway published the results of our years of conversations about careers and life. *Howard's Gift: Uncommon Wisdom to Inspire Your Life's Work*[14] seems to have hit a chord with people and has been translated into Korean, Chinese, and Japanese.

In day to day life, I'm disappointed if I don't get a chance to talk to each of my kids at least once a week. I appreciate a good book, enjoy watching NCIS and the History Channel on TV, and spend many happy hours working on my ever-expanding model train project.

"If you want to control a world, build a model railroad," I tell my friends.

I still play tennis doubles and just bought a new bike. At Fredi's urging, I have taken up golf. (As with the rest of life, I prefer to remember the good shots rather than the bad ones.) Fredi and I enjoy spending time with

---

13. *Getting to Giving: Fundraising the Entrepreneurial Way, by a Billion-Dollar Fundraiser*, Howard Stevenson with Shirley Spence, Timberline, 2011.
14. *Howard's Gift: Uncommon Wisdom to Inspire Your Life's Work*, Eric C. Sinoway with Merrill Meadow, St. Martin's Press, 2012.

our friends, and have subscriptions to the Red Sox, the Celtics, the ballet, and the symphony.

We love our Cambridge home. We enjoy spending time in Maine and Nonquitt, where we try to offer attractive distractions for family and other guests. We enjoy the occasional road trip to enjoy other parts of America.

Fredi also is involved in many important nonprofits including WBUR, The Smithsonian Institution National Board, SummerSearch, The Kennedy School Women's Leadership Board, the Museum of Science, Hestia, and the Cambridge Center for Adult Education. I play spouse at her events.

Still, time and a healthy respect for my heart's limitations have slowed things down a little. There is less global adventuring in my retirement than I imagined, but that is fine.

I've enjoyed my fair share of travel—Australia, Southeast Asia, China, India, The Middle East, Russia, Eastern and Western Europe, South America, Central America, Canada, and 47 states. I am missing Turkey, New Zealand and Greenland from my lifetime list, and not missing anything in Antarctica.

REFLECTIONS ON LIFE

I WAS A bit stumped when Shirley asked me for some reflections on my life; I don't do much of that because I believe in living life forward. She tried again: "Do you consider your life a success?" Ah, that one was easier.

The short answer is, "Yes!" I am very satisfied with my life.

I have an amazing wife, a family I'm proud of, and wonderful friends. I have a comfortable and enjoyable lifestyle. I like to think I'm leaving a little piece of the planet a bit better, for animal and man. Financially, I have exceeded my dreams many times over.

I have achieved some recognition in my field, although I am not someone who has done one thing forever. I have done a lot of things quite well, and I like to think that I had an impact on each. I was pleased by honors from Babson and a Doctorate *Honoris Causa* from The University of Montreal.

It has been a lot fun because there was so much variety: business, investing, academics and philanthropy. The most interesting thing, to me, is how that wide variety of activities interconnects across time and space, like a web.

By teaching entrepreneurship, I learned about investing. External relations led to fundraising. And so on. If you took out any one piece, my life would have been very different. It wasn't entirely by design either; I often say that I've had a serendipitous career.

These days, I am well aware of my own mortality but I don't really worry about it. I have done what I could and what I thought was right. I could sing along with Frank Sinatra, "I've lived a life that's full. I traveled each and ev'ry highway. And more, much more than this, I did it my way."

And now, what have I learned along the way?

LIVE AND LEARN: MY SIX TRUTHS

M Y SIX TRUTHS are a sort of "rules of the road" for my life journey but there is a reason why they appear at the end—not the beginning—of Part I; they have emerged over my 74 years, based on what has and hasn't worked in my experience. They are much easier to see in retrospect.

My truths are summarized in the box below and briefly described in the rest of this chapter. Collectively, they tell a story, my view of how the world works.

> **HOWARD'S SIX TRUTHS**
>
> 1. You are accountable for your actions and your life.
> 2. The one sure thing is that things will change.
> 3. You can never know all you need to know.
> 4. Predictions are guesses about the future.
> 5. Every action is a bet.
> 6. The house sets the rules; you decide whether to play.

I am accountable for my actions and my life. Life is full of uncertainties though, and I can't know everything I need to know to make good decisions. I compensate by predicting but predictions are just guesses, so every action is a bet in a game where I don't control the rules but I can decide if I want to play.

You may or may not agree with my six truths. That's fine; you get to decide your own truths. But they underlie much of what you will read in the rest of this book, so let's dissect them, truth by truth.

Truth 1—You Are Accountable for Your Actions and Your Life

The notion of personal accountability was engrained in me during my childhood. "Age of accountability" is a Mormon term referring to the age at which someone has the ability to know right from wrong, and the agency to do so. Agency, in turn, is defined as the ability to choose.

Mormons perform baptisms only after reaching the age of accountability, which is considered to be eight years old. I don't know if that's the right age but I do believe in the choice part of the premise, which makes each person responsible for his or her decisions and actions.

Your choices collectively will shape your life. You are living with the consequences of your previous decisions, and what you do today will have an impact on your future. Sometimes you can outsource a decision to others, but you still will be stuck with the consequences.

Taking effective action is the challenge and the opportunity, especially when many of the factors are beyond your control. A health condition may impose constraints or a global recession may decimate your job prospects. Most things in life involve other people too, which greatly complicates things.

You can muddle through life haphazardly but the better approach is to ask yourself, "What future do I want, and what's the best way to get there?" A dose of reality is important too; what futures are desirable *and* possible? Only that combination is a real opportunity.

I must admit that it upsets me when people don't take responsibility for their actions and their lives. It happens, however. Why is that?

One answer is the tendency to blame others for your problems, which gives you an excuse not to take action. (Politicians are especially proficient at that, as we see all too often.) Blaming obstacles is just another form of blaming others.

Learned helplessness—"I can't do it!"—is another problem. I know people who were raised that way. It often manifests itself in careers, where someone is sitting at the top of a little hill and can see the bigger hill, but is fearful of going through the valley. Taking action requires a measure of courage.

Truth 2—The One Sure Thing is That Things Will Change

I believe that the world is in constant change, and there is plenty of evidence to back that up. That truth is one reason why looking back at age 80, you may find that you have not ended up exactly where you imagined you would be.

Consider an 80-year-old American man today.

When he was born, his life expectancy was 59 years.[15] There were no fax machines or Internet. India was a British colony. The United States was the world's largest oil producer. General Motors and Ford dominated the world automotive industry. Space travel and nuclear weapons were science fiction.

I can't begin to imagine what my four-year-old granddaughter will experience over the course of her lifetime. I do know that—to survive and thrive—adaptability, lifelong learning, and a sense of adventure will be essential.

The more predictable changes in life, which are the best kind, are associated with life stages.

Shakespeare, in *As You Like It*, offers his version in an "All the world's a stage" soliloquy. People, he says, are mere players, making entrances and exits in a play with seven acts: infancy, adolescence, young adulthood, middle age, old age and death.

My version, crafted for a HBS 35th reunion talk, posits that we move through three distinct periods: the Go-Go, Slow-Go, and No-Go years. Each brings changes in "the three F's": functioning, finances and family. They are more psychological and physical than time bound.

The Go-Go years are typically marked by a feeling of immortality. Health, energy and future possibilities abound. Then the Slow-Go years begin. (It is said that if you are over the age of 50 and nothing hurts when you wake up, you are dead.) Careers, family, financial and personal needs are changing.

---

15. "Expectation of Life at Birth by Race and Sex: 1900 to 2001," U.S. Census Bureau, Statistical Abstract of the United States: 2003.

(I have entered the Slow-Go stage, with delusions of still being in my Go-Go years.)

The No-Go years are not something most people look forward to, except when they contemplate the alternative. The goal is to have each day be as good as it can be, but you don't buy green bananas or young fine Bordeaux wines.[16]

There inevitably will be surprises in life too—good and bad.

When I unexpectedly found myself a single father, I decided to leave Baupost. Had I stayed, I'd probably be worth a lot more. There's a wince factor there but no regrets. (If I had made that choice, many other successes would not have been possible.) I don't believe in regrets as a rule, so long as the decision process is sound.

The uncertainty of change isn't just about major decisions or long-term developments. It's about what may or may not happen in the next minute or hour. I thought I was in fine health on January 3, 2007, . . . until my heart stopped on that stroll across the HBS campus.

Truth 3—You Can Never Know All You Need to Know

As I've grown older, I've come to understand and accept how little I know and how little any of us can really know, no matter how long we live or how much we study. Being deluged daily with information (and misinformation) presented as truth actually exacerbates the problem.

This realization has a number of interesting side effects.

One is an increased sense of humility and awe, and curiosity about our ever-changing world. However, you also can develop a certain amount of cynicism about what you hear and are told, especially by so-called experts. (I am a fan of healthy cynicism, as I expect you've noticed by now.)

That cynicism can extend to the common wisdom, in our educational system, that good analysis will get you the right answer. Waiting for perfect information can easily result in "analysis paralysis." You could wait forever, and someone else would seize the opportunity.

Finally, there is an increased appreciation for the dilemma that we each face in all aspects of our lives; we have to make decisions and act without

---

16. Atul Gawande recently wrote a wonderful book called *Being Mortal: Medicine and What Matters in the End* (Metropolitan Books, 2014). He strongly advocates realism.

really knowing what the outcome may be. (And remember, there are some 7 billion other people out there doing the same thing.)

We resolve that dilemma by implicitly or explicitly making predictions. But as Sam Goldwyn said, "It's tough to predict, especially about the future." Oliver Wendell Holmes put it this way, "Every year, if not every day, we have to wager our salvation upon some prophecy based upon imperfect knowledge."

Truth 4—Predictions Are Guesses about the Future

Modern neuroscience increasingly shows that people are predicting machines. It's a basic survival skill (Is that rustling in the bushes a predator or lunch?) and how we cope with uncertainty. It's basically a three step process for reckoning what will happen next—observation, calculation and action.

Uncertainty creates anxiety, however, so people often try to present predictions as facts. Throughout history, fortune tellers in various guises have played important roles in guiding kings, politicians and ordinary folk. Many modern experts are skilled at making irrefutable statements.[17]

Take the weatherman who predicts a 30% chance of rain: If it rains, he was right; if it doesn't rain, he was right. We will never have ten identical days to test whether each time he says "30%" three out of ten days will have rain.

I tend to think of a prediction more as what Karl Popper would call a falsifiable proposition or a testable theory.[18] What are the confirming data? What signal can I get that I was wrong about my prediction? It's a useful way to think about all manner of things, from stock picking to GPS driving directions.

Our need for predictability isn't really a need for guarantees. People like games of chance where there are rules and calculable probabilities of achieving one of a known set of outcomes, and they can weigh the odds. Business and life are messier than that, of course, but the analogy is a good one.

---

17. One wag noted that the word expert has two parts: *ex* as in "has been" and *spurt* as a drip under pressure.
18. Karl Popper is the twentieth century philosopher of science who introduced falsifiability as the "solution" to problems with induction and universal generalizations.

Predicting is a helpful tool for navigating life, and you can improve your predictive intelligence. Some predictions are better than others but always remember: No one knows the future with certainty. Predictions are guesses, not facts.

Truth 5—Every Action Is a Bet

Whether you think of yourself as risk averse or a high roller, you are continuously taking actions in anticipation of future results. You're looking for good bets.

How do you decide whether it's a good bet? You have to look at three things: the upside (what's the best case scenario?), the downside (what's the worst case scenario?) and the odds (what are the probabilities of the various outcomes?).

You place your bet and see what happens. You may or may not get the desired result. The bet may change too, as time passes and circumstances change. You gather information and reassess; a new or different action may be warranted.

Investing is the easiest place to apply the betting analogy. Decisions about life and raising kids are more complicated, but the betting analysis still can be useful. One example: career choices.

Breaking into the country music business is many a singer's dream, although the odds of stardom are slim. If you're twenty years old and fresh out of school, you have little to lose. (Go for it!) Ten years later, married and with a new baby, the downside of a bad career is much higher. (Maybe not . . .)

There are a number of common betting errors that people make:

- *Overestimating the downside of change*—It's easy to do. The saying goes that "the only thing that likes to be changed is a wet baby."

- *Not seeing the option value of something new*—My attitude is: What can I learn? What new avenues will open up?

- *Forgetting that you can make a good bet and still lose*—You have to have a Plan B and be willing to say "I was wrong." When you're in a hole, stop digging.

People thought I was crazy when I turned down tenure at HBS but I saw no downside (I could get another job) and a huge potential upside (avoiding the velvet-lined rut). The Dean's suggestion that I "do something important" (i.e., other than real estate) also made it clear who was writing the rules.

Truth 6—The House Sets the Rules; You Decide Whether to Play

In gambling, the casino sets the betting limits and the black jack table has its own rules. In investing, there are SEC rules, fund managers, and deal term sheets. In life, the house may be the college you're applying to, the company you're working for, or even your own family.

The house always has rules, usually set to its own advantage. Your challenge, as the bettor, is to understand the rules. The big question is: Is this a game you want to play? If you can't figure out the rules, my advice is to walk.

If you *are* able to figure them out, there are a series of questions to ask yourself: Do the rules give the house an unfair advantage? Is there any way for me to gain some control over the rules? (How) can I use the rules to my advantage?

The rules of the game may be written by others, but you can learn to play the game and use the rules to your advantage. I figured that out early in life.

When I was a kid, I entered a Chrysler "rodeo contest" where you had to drive through a maze without knocking down the balls at each curve. I walked through the maze first and decided to crush a few on purpose, to allow for a straight shot through the rest. It worked; I came in second statewide.

Rules can be tricky. They can be implicit as well as explicit. Many are not written down and most are subject to interpretation. Rules aren't chiseled in stone, either. Sometimes they are renegotiated by the players in a deal. Often they are changed by forces in the outside environment.

If you don't like the house's rules, you may be able to find a house with fairer rules. If you can't, you're back to that line in the sand: Is this a game you want to be playing, on this house's terms?

So there you have it, my six truths. A final truth, however, might be that there have been plenty of missteps where I thought I knew more than I did or I thought I could change the rules of the game. Learning is a lifelong task.

With that as a backdrop, let's move on to Part II and the subject of wealth—how to think about it, how to build it, and how to manage it.

BUILDING AND MANAGING WEALTH

WEALTH IS A tricky thing. The basic idea is to grow, preserve, and transfer wealth but it quickly gets complicated.

There are a host of activities and players involved, and endless decisions over the course of a lifetime. It's not just the technical issues either, or the fact that there's a good dose of luck involved. There is an emotional side to wealth too.

As one of my daughters (who is a marriage and family therapist) explained, money has an emotional meaning for each of us that was modeled by our parents and is a component of our close relationships as adults. Sharing your feelings about money, she notes, is important for healthy relationships.[19]

Part II of this book is my effort to explain how I feel and think about wealth, and what I've learned about building and managing it.

We'll start by considering the nature and dynamics of wealth in *Chapter 4*, and then describe my approach to wealth management in *Chapter 5*. *Chapter 6* will share what I think I know about investing. We'll close with some advice for getting and using professional help, in *Chapter 7*.

---

19. For more details, see *http://trevorcrow.com/money-and-relationships/*.

NATURE AND DYNAMICS OF WEALTH

WEALTH MEANS DIFFERENT things to different people, as evidenced by the quotes we found from across centuries, continents and cultures. (See the *Appendix*.) My most recent inspiration came from a sign in a café in Wilmington, North Carolina: "The best things in life aren't things."

So, let's start with a basic question: What is wealth? There are some interesting variations in the traditional definitions of wealth. At the risk of what may seem like hairsplitting, we'll review some of them, and then take a look at my views on the subject.

TRADITIONAL DEFINITIONS OF WEALTH

BUSINESS DICTIONARY'S DEFINITION offers three different slants. In general, *wealth is something that makes a person, family, or group better off*. Accounting-wise, *wealth is assets minus liabilities*. From an economics perspective, *wealth is the total of all assets that generate current income or have the potential to generate future income*.

Good old Webster's Dictionary offers a more succinct definition of wealth as *an abundance of valuable material possessions or resources*. But I wonder, How much is "abundant?"

Wikipedia offers an answer: *An individual who is considered wealthy, affluent, or rich is someone who has accumulated substantial wealth relative to others in society or their reference group.*

I have some problems with each of those definitions.

Let's start with Wikipedia's notion that wealth is a relative thing. I might agree about comparing an individual's actual wealth relative to his wealth expectations; a windfall can leave you feeling rich. But comparing yourself to what others have accumulated isn't very helpful, in my experience.

I have a multimillionaire friend who much of the time feels poor . . . compared to Bill Gates. Several of my friends have over a hundred times what I have, yet I have created wealth that is a hundred times what most people have amassed. How should I feel? (For the record, I feel just fine.)

Another problem is that most definitions don't deal with the expenditure side or cash flow issues. A basketball superstar may burn through $5.5 million a year for five years, and then see his career and spending power come to a screeching halt.

Having complained about the standard definitions, here are some ways that I have come to think about the nature and dynamics of wealth.

MY DEFINITION OF WEALTH

Wealth is a storehouse of value and future possibilities.

THERE ARE THREE kinds of stock in the storehouse of value. (I don't mean stocks as in NASDAQ or the NYSE; I am using the term broadly here.) Some grow in value, some sustain their value, and others diminish in value.

Let's start with the fun one: *growth stocks*.

Albert Einstein sometimes is quoted as saying, "Compound interest is the eighth wonder of the world. He who understands it, earns it . . . he who doesn't . . . pays it." Did he say that, really? We can't find the source but it doesn't matter; the point is valid. Compounding is a powerful thing.

American Research and Development (ARD)'s investment in Digital Equipment Corporation (DEC) is a dramatic example.

In 1957, ARD invested $70,000 in Olsen and Anderson's start-up. In 1968, following DEC's initial public offering, ARD shares were worth $355 million.[20] Many believe that is the best investment ever made since Queen Isabella backed Christopher Columbus to abscond with the treasures of the new world.

---

20. "American Research Development Corp," Entrepreneurial MIT (*http://museum.mit.edu/150/78*).

Compounding occurs not just with interest bearing accounts but also with a growing business or real estate that is increasing in value. An easy trap to fall into, however, is failing to address the question of whether something really is growing in value or simply benefiting from a bubble or inflation.

Sustaining stocks are hard to find.

Many people view real estate as a sustaining investment. The founder of Bessemer Securities is reported to have said, "The good thing about real estate is that when you shouldn't sell it, you can't possibly."

I think that TONE (Timber Owners of New England), which is one of our family investments, offers a good example of a sustaining stock. It neither gives current yield nor requires funds to maintain. Here's how it works with TONE.

TONE has over 3,000 acres in Southern New Hampshire with lots of trees, five houses, several ponds, and a complicated relationship with a group that has a license to use the houses. We own over one-third. I've been involved since 1971, and serve as treasurer. Two of my sons sit on the board.

The trees grow, and then are cut and sold. The income keeps the houses in repair, the caretaking done, the roads open, and the timber operations running. A pejorative view is that TONE is in the land of the living dead. A more positive view is that it is holding its own and waiting for good things to happen.

At a minimum, I think that TONE gives our family access to an increasingly unique resource. Our investment is relatively small and TONE is cash flow positive. Unlike with direct ownership of property, we don't have to put cash in or be worried when there is a big storm; that's someone else's problem.

The third type of stocks is *diminishing* assets, things that will depreciate in value over time.

One major concern I have is when people confuse diminishing assets with growing or sustaining stocks. When people talk of investing in clothes, jewelry, art or other possessions, I want to scream, "Watch out!"

If you own Tsarina Alexandra's tiara, an original Chanel dress in mint condition, or the work of a hot artist, you might say that I am crazy. But jewelry is melted down for the gold, that dress won't last forever, and Andres Zorn has fallen from his exalted place as an artist in 1910.

I am not against jewelry or other niceties; I just don't carry them on my personal balance sheet.

I try not to forget that each purchase involves transaction, opportunity and carrying costs. It's usually best to view them as consumption expenditures, not investments. They may benefit from future perceptions of their value and from inflation, but don't count on it.

By the way, I am not alone in my skepticism.

In an article about the "murkily defined asset class" called art, *Grant's Interest Rate Observer* noted that works by unproven, contemporary artists "can bring an arm, a leg and a torso," while rare historical documents often go begging. "You begin to wonder about the meaning of money," it marveled.[21]

Indeed.

There are other ways to think about wealth, of course. Most presentations like to remind you that wealth is tangible and intangible. That is true but oversimplified, and of limited use in thinking about the value of different kinds of wealth. I see it more as a spectrum, as illustrated in **Figure 4-1**.

FIGURE 4-1
A Wealth Spectrum

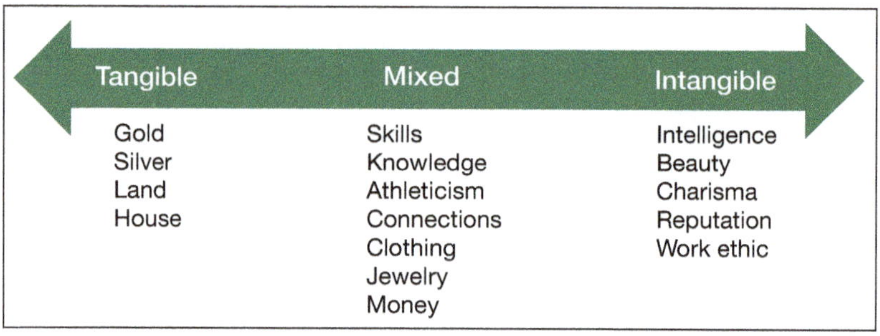

Tangible	Mixed	Intangible
Gold	Skills	Intelligence
Silver	Knowledge	Beauty
Land	Athleticism	Charisma
House	Connections	Reputation
	Clothing	Work ethic
	Jewelry	
	Money	

Where to position the various kinds of wealth is highly debatable. And assessing their value? That's even harder, and greatly depends on the context. Let's look at some examples:

- ◆ Beauty is a classic intangible asset but good looks may be a hard asset if you model for a living. (The definition of good looks, by the way, will depend on who is doing the looking.)

---

21. "Short Koons, Long Lincoln," *Grant's Interest Rate Observer*, Vol. 31, No. 17, September 6, 2013.

- Clothing keeps you warm and "decent" but a bikini at a beach is different from a bikini at a ball, never mind a nudist's camp. And the expression "Clothes make the man" is often taken to the extreme: "Fake it until you make it."

- Intelligence may be valuable but in what form: emotional, spatial, numerical or physical? Each is useful for different things; think software engineer versus therapist versus car mechanic. (One day, lost in the Guatemalan countryside, I decided that I had no useful skills for survival.)

- Harvard enjoys great prestige, but—as Harvard Union workers seeking wage increases pointed out—you can't eat prestige. The same could be said for gold; it may be a classic tangible asset but it will be useless to someone alone in the desert, dying of thirst.

We could go on, but you get the point.

Sometimes one form of wealth can be exchanged for another, more attractive one; sometimes not. Tuition money can buy you education for a high paying career. Trying to buy a good reputation is an almost hopeless hope although in today's celebrity culture, money can get you notoriety.

Most wealth presentations, by the way, usually turn pretty quickly to money. We don't live in a barter society, and money is the ultimate fungible asset. Still, I keep a 100 trillion Zimbabwe dollar bill as a reminder that even hard cash is only as good as the faith people have in it. (See **Figure 4-2**).

FIGURE 4-2
Zimbabwe Currency—Suspended in 2009

Closer to home, the price of gold dropped from $1,855 in 2011 to $1,078 at last check, and house values fell 25% in the 2007–2009 time frame. Would that make Treasury bills a better choice for your storehouse of value? They might be, unless interest rates change or inflation speeds up.

It's not as simple as it seems, and the best bet probably is to keep your wealth in different kinds of assets. Diversification is a fundamental principle of investing and wealth management.

Finally, as we've said before and will say again, it's not all about the money. Much has been written on that, but we'll settle here for a few tongue-in-cheek observations from Dilbert and friends.

DILBERT © 1996 Scott Adams. Used By permission of UNIVERSAL UCLICK. All rights reserved

DILBERT © 1989 Scott Adams. Used By permission of UNIVERSAL UCLICK. All rights reserved.

Now, let's take a closer look at the dynamics of wealth.

WEALTH DYNAMICS

Wealth creation is about the present and future value of money, the accumulation of a pool of assets.

THE DYNAMICS OF wealth is an incredibly important subject for you and your life partner to agree upon, and to try to teach your children. In theory, it's quite simple. In practice, it gets complicated very quickly.

Here's the secret: Wealth is like a flywheel.[22] It takes a lot of effort to get started but once it's turning, there's kinetic energy. It will keep going, building reserves that can be tapped into as needed.

The flows in and out of your pool of assets are perhaps the most important consideration in wealth because they are actionable. (See **Figure 4-3**.) If the inflows exceed the outflows, your pool of assets grows and you are building for the future. If the opposite is true, you are borrowing from the future.

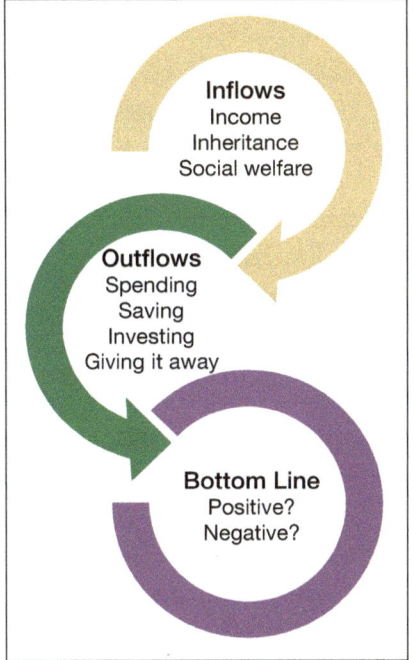

FIGURE 4-3
Wealth Flows

WEALTH INFLOWS

OF THE THREE inflows—income, inheritance, and social welfare—income is the only inflow you can control, and that will be the focus of our discussion here. (Inheritance will come up many times in coming chapters.) You can generate income by earning a paycheck, building a business and/or investing.

---

22. A flywheel is a mechanical device used to store rotational energy (e.g., for use in automobile engines).

Earned Income

Finding a way to use your time and talents in a way that will cause others to part with their money is important, I believe. Your skills may be in commerce, the arts, athletics, medicine, teaching or any number of other areas. A salary can be a seen as recognition that you are doing something of value.

That said, too many people take salary as a measure of personal worth. Salaries tend to be industry specific so it's not a useful comparison, except perhaps as a commentary on social values. No school teacher will make as much as the average investment banker.

Most people, however, want to compare their salaries with others. That becomes an almost impossible problem for the employer and does little for the individual. As an employee, the question for me always was, "Am I in the market range for what I am producing for my organization?"

The velvet-lined rut of a high paying job is a notorious trap. If you find yourself thinking, "I'm miserable but I'm making a lot of money," you might want to look for other ways to accomplish your goals. (It helps to be clear on your goals; we'll come back to that.)

Finally, earned income is the lightweight in the flywheel equation. As soon as you stop getting that paycheck, earned income goes away. There's no momentum. You are constrained to what you get paid for doing a job. Basically, you're exchanging your labor in order to satisfy your needs.

Still, if you have nothing, you have to start there. You may find that you are happy as an employee. And even if you want to work for yourself, working for someone else first can be a tremendous learning opportunity. (One of my sons claims that management consulting was where he learned how not to manage.)

Business Income

Business income is simply an extension of earned income; you work and others work for you. As the owner of a business, I leverage my employees' time and talents. My income is not restricted to my own efforts.[23]

My employees are in effect exchanging some of the benefits of their production for other values, such as financial security or camaraderie.

---

[23]. You can extend this argument to nonprofit organizations, where being higher up in the hierarchy may mean you're better paid, but you still rely on others to deliver value.

Everyone must feel that they are better off through the exchange, to create a sustainable organization.

The benefit to being the boss is that even when I'm not productive, others (hopefully) are. If the task of managing employees consumes too much time and energy, however, my productivity may fall. And if no surplus is produced to be split, there is negative leverage on my time. It's not a free lunch.

Business income is not purely a function of the time and talent invested either. Often you have to invest money as well, and the results are a mixture of return on effort and return on capital. If you don't distinguish between the two, there is great danger that you are cheating at solitaire.

It's also important not to confuse a real business with a hobby. You have to be honest about the economics whether it's a horse farm, a winery or—yes—writing a book. Sometimes there are tax implications to consider; is your home office a personal expense or a business deduction?

Investment Income

Investment gains are characterized by some politicians and polemicists as "unearned income." There seems to be a feeling among some that investment returns just fall from the sky. My experience is that achieving above average returns over time requires skill and hard work as well as luck.

Investment income represents the flow generated from the surplus that you (or someone else) has accumulated, from your (or their) labor or business. With success, that surplus generates its own flows as a continuing stream of interest and rents or in a tax-advantaged way though long term capital gains.

Investing is a leveraged activity.

When I started my personal investing, I used my talent, the bank's money and a rising economy to create economic value. When we started Baupost, we leveraged our reputation, investment, and fundraising skills, and favorable stock market and interest rate conditions to create value for ourselves and our clients.

Admittedly, investment income can be confusing. Sometimes there is little cash flow but the value increases as potential distributions (dividends) are reinvested. Sometimes the distributions exceed the value being currently generated, in which case the value goes down in a long-term liquidation process.

Which Is Right for You?

We've considered three ways to make money. How do you figure out what's right for you? Eric Sinoway captured much of what I have to say about career planning in *Howard's Gift*, so I'll point you there. For now, though, here are a few observations and words of advice.

My own wealth came from all three types of income, though not in equal measure and each at different stages of my life. I derived great satisfaction from my paid work but I craved independence, which led me elsewhere. I was always looking for opportunities to leverage my time and talent.

Whatever path you pursue, choices will be required.

What is more important to you: work that you enjoy, work with impact on society, personal economics, or control over your time? Your parameters will change, especially as you go from just worrying about yourself to the demands of a family.

You can expect conflicts among the goals, and you will need to learn how to juggle competing priorities, which can be stressful. One critical skill is to be able to shift from work mode to home mode. Other tips are to relax with friends, and use small amounts of time to calm yourself (e.g., try shutting your eyes in an elevator).

Another common problem is that high income often generates high expenses. It's easy to get seduced by an expensive lifestyle that you can't really afford, or leaves nothing for the future. I am amazed at how little money many investment bankers have saved during boom periods.

One approach is to try to gain control of your financial destiny by starting or buying a business, if you can. It's important to recognize that you're not making an investment, however; it's a commitment. Think ham and eggs breakfast. The chicken is invested but the pig is committed.

For many people, the psychological commitment, stress and risk of entrepreneurship are perceived as too great; they find that working for and with others is better for them. That's fine. Not everyone wants to be a boss. The one area where that wish can never be fulfilled is in your investment life.

Some involvement in investing becomes almost inevitable once you've accumulated a certain level of wealth. Will you get directly involved or find someone that you trust to manage your money? Even if you opt to delegate, you are accountable for your financial future. (More on that later.)

My last bit of income advice is to take a total return approach to inflows. Consider all sources and be flexible as circumstances change. Your expenditures don't care where the money comes from, but you need to pay attention because each form of income has different characteristics and certainties.

You could, of course, factor the two non-income inflows—inheritance and social welfare—into your wealth equation, but I would advise caution.

You may or may not inherit something, even if you think you will. The government may or may not come through with promised Social Security and Medicare benefits, and is as likely as not to tax you on them. Both are beyond your control.

Now, about those expenditures . . .

WEALTH OUTFLOWS

OUTFLOWS BASICALLY ARE about consumption, current and deferred. You can spend, save, invest or give away your resources. It's important to be clear on which is which, to make good decisions. But the lines can be blurry and may shift with changing circumstances, as we'll see below.

Spending

Spending is consumption for current pleasure. I don't think that people think enough about their spending. It's important to recognize fixed versus variable costs, and to make conscious choices about expenditures. I'm not talking about just the big spending decisions either. Look at the everyday ones too. Ask yourself questions like these:

- Is that purchase a necessity or just a habit?
- Do I really want this or am I just following the crowd?
- How do I reward myself for success?
- How do I want to spend my time?

The answers will be highly personal, of course, and likely will change with time. I am happy to share some of the ways I have come to think about spending, as one case example.

My upbringing contributed to what I consider a healthy attitude towards parting with my hard earned cash. My sons think I'm cheap, and I'm proud of that. That doesn't mean that I don't enjoy nice things, however, or that I am not generous. What does it mean then?

To start, I want to know that I am getting value for money when I buy something; I hate to waste money. The other big question always is: What am I spending that gives me and the people that I care about pleasure?

I get my Brooks Brothers shirts at the outlet store. I drive a Lincoln but don't need the latest model. I feel a tad extravagant using those Keurig single serve coffee cups, and mentally add the cost of gas to my Starbucks purchase price. I worry about how much I spend for cable boxes that are rarely used.

I enjoy wine but my pleasure is in finding a good buy. I'm looking for a $15 bottle that tastes as good as or better than a $60 buy, especially after it has aged. Occasionally I have to step it up for certain guests (some people really do care about the label) but that is a different problem.

When it comes to rewards for success, my home is important to me. I've had nice houses relative to my net worth my whole life. That's how I grew up plus I wanted a home that I could enjoy and a place for the kids to roam. Still, I always asked myself, "If the value of the house went to zero, would it kill me?"

I've always admired Porsches too, but it wasn't until 1998 that I succumbed to the pleasure of one. At that point, it represented a very small percentage of my net worth. I still have it. (Like me, it is becoming an antique and I have many more miles on me than the 24,000 miles on the car's odometer).

(Both of those examples—houses and cars—raise that pesky problem of being disciplined about which kind of outflow is which: expenditure or investment? We'll come back to that later.)

I don't especially enjoy security lines at the airport or a cramped seat (I usually fly coach with Jet Blue's extra legroom) but I have no desire to own or charter a private plane. The trick—as with yachts and other big toys—is to know someone who has one.

That example brings us to the time versus money trade-off.

I like knowing how to fix things, partly for convenience and partly to save money. Time is a finite resource though and there are many skills that I lack, so sometimes a repairman is called. I will hire someone to mow the lawn, though I don't mind doing it.

Saving and Investing

Saving and investing take money from current consumption in anticipation of future uses.

Young people are routinely advised to start saving and investing early, to reap the rewards of compounding. That can be hard though because it's about deferred gratification. Allow me to offer a few tricks that I've developed over the years, to make it easier.

Here's one: Don't create money in a form that makes it easy to spend. I like to create value that doesn't burn a hole in my pocket.

As a young professor, choosing to serve on boards for stock options rather than doing high-priced consulting was one way to do that. My colleague got the Jaguar XKE (right away), but I made my first million (some years later, but first).

Here's another: When you get a windfall, stash it where you and ideally Uncle Sam can't get at it. When I inherited a bit of money from my grandmother in 1972, I left it in the trust for my sons. When I got my first big distribution from Baupost, I used part of it to set up a charitable trust.

(I love my kids, my grandkids, and even some grand dogs. I am less partial to my Uncle Sam, even though I regularly give him a substantial chunk of my income.)

Now, that problem of true investments versus phony investments. Distinguishing between consumption expenditures and investments can be hard, as we saw earlier, even if you're trying to be rigorously honest. There are lots of judgment calls involved.

When it comes to cars, I see them as depreciating assets, not investments. I finance them to remind myself of that, even when I could pay outright. I also want to think of them as transportation, not status symbols. I like my cars safe, reliable and generally inconspicuous (the Porsche aside).

I don't mind if they are fast. I rationalize that as a safety feature for when I want to pass on a two lane rural road. I have never come close to the top speed on any of my cars, but acceleration is fun and satisfying when you're behind a big, slow truck.

I also think carefully about mortgage payments.

When I had to borrow money to buy a house, I considered mortgage payments consumption expenses, an alternative to rent payments. Today I could pay off my mortgage but prefer to use it as a tax efficient way to leverage my portfolio. It's like borrowing money at 2.78% from the bank, which I then can reinvest for a better return.

Giving It Away

Giving is about fulfilling obligations, real or perceived. It can take a number of forms: tax payments to the government, philanthropy, and helping family members and other individuals. It's a habit that can be developed early; you don't have to be rich to offer a helping hand.

There can be many motivations for philanthropic giving. I will refer you to *Getting to Giving* for a more in-depth look at that question. Personally, the ability to have an impact on things that I care about is one of the biggest benefits of wealth and psychic rewards of success. (It's not about the tax write-offs.)

Fredi and I get great pleasure out of philanthropy that helps to create a better world or a stronger community. We have donated approximately 20% of our joint net worth to philanthropy, in part through a charitable trust. (We also contribute our time, talents and networks.)

Then, there are gifts to individuals we care about.

I helped my aunt and uncle while they were alive, and still send a check every month to the woman who helped take care of Aunt Zola when she got Alzheimer's. I helped our cleaning lady with legal expenses for a nasty divorce, and paid for her daughter's college. I have helped more than one student.

Last but far from least, is family.

We'll talk much more about wealth and families in Part III. I do want to make the point here, however, that helping family members financially isn't all about inheritances.

I drew that lesson from a great-aunt who lived much more frugally than Grandmother Higginbotham, had one child and died wealthy at the age of 91. Her daughter (my second cousin), a childless retired schoolteacher, was stunned to learn that she had inherited $20 million. She spent the rest of her life trying to give it away.

My great-aunt made some significant contributions to her community through her daughter's philanthropy. Still, I can't help but wonder whether my second cousin might have made different choices in her own life, had she known about or had access to some of that wealth earlier on.

Fredi and I have tried to provide financial help to family members when they needed it. That practice will definitely create differences in their financial positions when we pass, but large inheritances later will not make up for lost opportunities in the present.

With inheritances, I believe that the beneficiaries should know the best estimates of their future. That knowledge creates opportunities to discuss ambitions, goals and dreams. I always told my children that I could give them choices but they had to earn their own success (and success wasn't a balance sheet).

As I mentioned earlier, I don't particularly love my Uncle Sam. On the other hand, I recognize that our family's success over multiple generations has depended on the benefits derived from our community: education, safety, infrastructure, freedoms, etc. I view my income taxes as repayment of that debt.

For some reason, I view estate taxes differently. Perhaps it's the feeling that I have already paid taxes as I accumulated wealth and therefore shouldn't be penalized for prudence. I've worked hard to minimize estate taxes and have been able to reduce taxable assets by over 70%.

My solution to the estate tax problem as well as the inheritor knowledge problem has been to make transfers early. With income taxes, I took the optimistic view that my taxable income would not be going down, and wanted to pay taxes currently rather than defer them.

THE BOTTOM LINE

THERE IS MUCH wisdom in what my sons claim to be a Stevenson family motto: "Being rich is spending less than you make. Being poor is spending more than you make." Simple but not easy.

How will you measure your financial success? Figuring out your scorecard is one example of the challenges of wealth management. There are many ways to attack the problem. Read on, for my approach.

MY APPROACH TO WEALTH MANAGEMENT

MOST OF THE wealthy people I know are better at making money than managing it. In this chapter, I'll offer my perspective on wealth management, and illustrate it with a personal case study. It may not be right for you but it has served me (and my family) quite well.

MY PERSPECTIVE ON WEALTH MANAGEMENT

THE SEVEN PRINCIPLES summarized in the box below reflect my overall philosophy and offer some core practices for effectively managing wealth. They flow from my six truths and have evolved over the years.

> **HOWARD'S WEALTH MANAGEMENT PRINCIPLES**
>
> 1. Wealth is a responsibility.
> 2. Wealth is an instrument of choice.
> 3. Good choices require good goals.
> 4. It's a three-legged stool.
> 5. Scorecards matter.
> 6. Enough is enough.
> 7. Fail to plan, and you plan to fail.

Principle 1—Wealth Is a Responsibility

Truth 1—you are accountable for your actions and your life—extends to your financial responsibilities, even (perhaps especially) if you rely on others for help. The central question is: Who are you responsible for?

First and foremost, you are responsible for yourself. If that sounds selfish, it's not. You don't want to be a burden on others. (The best gift you can give your kids is to be financially secure for retirement, according to one family wealth advisor.)

From there, it's about who else you are financially responsible for, when and how. The first question to ask yourself is: Who and what do I care about?

For me, the answer is community, which I see as a series of concentric circles. Family is at the core, then the people who have helped me, and then local and broader communities. Still, there are lots of choices to be made there; no one's wealth is infinite.

When it comes to family, I believe that I am most responsible for my spouse and young kids, those dependent on me. As my children grow up, I try to help them achieve their goals, so they can be responsible for themselves and the next generation.

A final point is that wealth can be a two-edged sword. You can use it to empower people, which is very satisfying. But wealth also can be misused—inadvertently or on purpose—as an instrument of control. (More on that in Part III.)

Principle 2—Wealth Is an Instrument of Choice

Wealth, as a storehouse of value and future possibilities, offers those of us who have it a wonderful thing—choices.

Wealth can buy you flexibility in making educational, career and a host of other life decisions. The freedom to make your own choices can be an important motivator for building wealth. That definitely was true in my case, as you saw in my life story.

Living in a world full of opportunities, however, can be a mixed blessing. I have watched many a HBS student paralyzed by too many choices, fearful of making the wrong one and "ruining" his or her life. I try to share a different way of looking at it, to unfreeze their thinking.

At any point in time, you have a range of possibilities before you. Whatever choice you make will close off some options, but also may open up some unforeseen ones. You may not end up exactly where you imagined you would be, but you likely will be quite satisfied or even pleasantly surprised.

There is some peril to not having a destination for your journey, however, as illustrated by this exchange between Alice and the Cheshire Cat, in *Alice's Adventures in Wonderland*:[24]

> *"Would you tell me, please, which way I ought to go from here?"* said Alice.
>
> *"That depends a good deal on where you want to get to,"* said the Cat.
>
> *"I don't much care where—"* said Alice.
>
> *"Then it doesn't matter which way you go,"* said the Cat.
>
> *"—so long as I get SOMEWHERE,"* Alice added as an explanation.
>
> *"Oh, you're sure to do that,"* said the Cat, *"if you only walk long enough."*

Principle 3—Good Choices Require Good Goals

At their most expansive, goals are a vision for your future. Henry Thoreau sums it up nicely in *Walden*: "I learned this . . . that if one advances confidently in the direction of his dreams and endeavors to live the life which he has imagined, he will meet with a success unexpected in the common hours."

Here's another good quote, courtesy of my friend Patrick Liles: "Just because a gun sounds, do not start running. Ask where the race is going." One of my professors claimed he was so competitive that he had to be first at the dump on Saturday morning. Competition is fine, but to what end is the question.

---

24. The paraphrased version is "If you don't know where you're going, any road will get you there."

In *Howard's Gift,* we talked about how it is sometimes easier when you start at the end. With certain long term goals, many short term decisions make no sense. To choose a simple example, if the goal is financial independence, then spending more than you make is nonsense.

Goal setting also requires a certain level of self-awareness. BBCL students began their life planning process with exercises that probed issues like: How do I define success? What are my core values? What are my strengths and weaknesses? What relationships are important to me?[25]

Setting goals can be hard because life consists of a number of interacting domains: career, family, community and self. You will need to make continuous trade-offs: This or that? Now or later? Many people talk of balance but it's more like juggling.

If you think of the parts of life as balls, the important questions are: Which balls are crystal and will shatter if dropped? Which ones are rubber and will bounce, hopefully to be caught on the rebound? Relationships are more likely to be the crystal balls. Financial ambitions will probably bounce.

Principle 4—It's a Three-legged Stool

Goals are one leg of what I think of as a three-legged stool for growing, preserving and transferring wealth; the other two are structure and people.

I give credit to Tom Rogerson who, as a financial speaker to HBS alumni groups, taught me the importance of thinking about the purposes of wealth and structuring your assets accordingly. Using the right pocket makes a huge difference.

Depending on your goals, you may choose to structure your assets in a variety of ways. Options include cash, stock, property, pensions, 401Ks, life insurance, trusts, private foundations, holding structures (e.g., limited partnerships), and more. Each comes in many flavors, with many people eager to "help."

Let's take trusts as an example. A trust basically is a fiduciary relationship where one party (the trustor) gives another party (the trustee) the right to hold property or assets for the benefit of a third party (the beneficiary).

---

25. As explained in Chapter 2, BBCL (Building a Business in the Context of a Life) was a HBS course taught by Howard. It required MBA students to write a personal life plan with financial scenarios.

Trusts can fulfill a variety of goals including estate planning, charitable giving, legal protection of property (e.g., against lawsuits or divorce), tax avoidance, funding your retirement, placing different kinds of assets in different hands, and control (e.g., "incentive trusts").

For the trustor, the basic questions are: Who do I want to get what? When? How much am I willing and able to pay in taxes now? Answering those questions can get complicated pretty quickly, however.

There are many different types of trusts with many different names depending on their purpose (e.g., generation skipping trusts, to get assets to the grandkids) or characteristics (e.g., absolute or discretionary distribution). The complexity is compounded by the fact that rules vary by state.

Then, there are more tough questions, even for a simple trust: Who to name as trustees, and how much power to give them?

Lawyers and bankers are common but ill-advised choices because they'll charge you for legal services as well as trust supervision, and may not have your best interests at heart. (One bank trustee was not making any distributions to a widow because it was more tax efficient to leave the money in the bank.)

I prefer to ask friends whose judgment I respect to serve as trustees. I have set up my son Andy as administrative trustee, to save them the burden of paperwork. I also have established a group of overseers, whose sole power is to fire a trustee and hire a new one should something be amiss.

Principle 5—Scorecards Matter

Different people use different metrics including net income, margin, net worth and total wealth. How will you measure your financial success? Some metrics are better than others, in my view.

Many people focus on *net income*. I think that is just plain wrong because it says nothing about expenses and longevity.

Margin (i.e., expenses/revenues) is a more useful metric because it lets you know whether you are overspending. It is equivalent to the savings rate but the term makes me think about how risky and levered my lifestyle is.

Net worth is even better, taking into account the balance sheet effects of asset appreciation and depreciation, debt financing of purchases, and after tax cash flow. I regularly track personal and household net worth.

One of the challenges with calculating net worth is that gifts can make you feel badly. Is a gift to your spouse really a diminution of your success as measured by net worth? Proactive gifts to children, friends and charities have the same effect; your net worth goes down.

Total wealth—for the family—is the most meaningful metric for me. It doesn't aim to capture every family member's total assets, but it does include what I consider "created" assets—assets transferred from Fredi and me to others (e.g., trusts, housing purchases, charities).

I keep a scorecard that includes these gifts and even an estimate of current values. Yes, they are no longer "mine" but psychologically I can take some credit and not feel badly when my personal wealth declines.

Principle 6—Enough Is Enough

When asked about their financial goals, the average response of students in one BBCL class was $250 million. Yes, that was the amount "needed" *per person*. I understand the pressure of student loans, but really?! If that is their minimum, I foresee some disappointment in their futures.

Money is a continuous function down to the penny ($100 is less than $100.01) but I tend to think of it in quantum terms with different stages of needs and wants. Five dollars doesn't buy you much these days, except for a Quarter Pounder with cheese. To move from stage to stage requires a lot more.

- *Stage 1* is simply having enough food to eat. That is the main focus of a subsistence migrant worker and, in fact, a large percentage of our world's population.

- *Stage 2* is about having a roof over your head and basic education for your children. As soon as people have a steady income, this becomes a realistic goal.

- At *Stage 3*, people are less concerned about paying the rent, but still worry about job security and the unexpected costs of illness or unemployment. Toys and treats—cars, televisions, summer camp for the kids—become affordable luxuries.

- *Stage 4* is about owning your home. You start accumulating assets. Leverage is available and you may begin to think about retirement and college tuition for the kids. (More tough trade-offs.)

- With *Stage 5* come more and bigger toys and treats, maybe a boat or a motor home or a trip to Europe. Charitable contributions may increase.

- At *Stage 6,* it's about a second home, helping grown children, and upgrading your toys. Fancier cars, nicer clothing, jewelry and other things are possible, but you still can't have it all.

I have no experience beyond Stage 6, but I have observed that for some people, it then starts getting into things like having a private airplane, a great art collection, and very expensive watches and jewelry. For others, it inspires big philanthropy.

Now the big question: How much is enough?

It gets harder as you move through the stages because you get used to being comfortable. It also depends on where you start.

A wealthy friend's son was puzzled. Why, on a family trip, had they walked right through the first class section of the plane, where they usually sat? (Answer: It was sold out.) I'm not sure what that reaction portends for the son's future. I do hope that his inheritance is large and well managed.

Another problem is the tendency to compare ourselves to others. The wealthometer, which allows you to plug in your income and see where you rank, was an instant hit. I would wager that most people were looking up, not down, in the rankings.

The most important standard, I believe, is an internal one. You have to decide for yourself, how much is enough and what to do when you've attained that goal. By any reasonable standard, I am well off. I also know that, if need be, I could get by with fewer toys and treats, and be just fine.

Principle 7—Fail to Plan, and You Plan to Fail

That adage is attributed to Winston Churchill and Benjamin Franklin. General Eisenhower added, "Plans are nothing, planning is everything." I agree that planning really is more about the process than the output. "A good plan today is better than a perfect plan tomorrow" is another wise saying.

Will I be able to do what I want over a one or three or five year period? What is the right time frame to be using? Am I spending too much and saving too little? Who might I need to help? Who do I need to help me? What will I do if (*when*, really) my needs or circumstances change?

Planning helps you answer those questions, and think about the consequences if things go wrong. It requires long-term thinking but tempered with tactical responsiveness to the real world. You can backward induce from where you want to end up, to set financial goals for along the way.

You have to be realistic about where you are as well. You need a grasp of your financial realities—what you have, what you spend, and what you earn. Only then can you adjust your plans and your behaviors as needed to reach your goals.

Finally, don't forget Truth 2—Things will change. "Life is what happens to you while you're busy making other plans," is how John Lennon put it. You have to pay attention and be flexible.

What happens when you follow my wealth management principles? I will offer up my own experience as a case study, adding some color commentary to what you have read in previous chapters.

A WEALTH MANAGEMENT CASE STUDY

LET'S START WITH life goals.

I never sat down and wrote an essay about what I would do with "my one wild and precious life."[26] (That was one of the exercises we asked BBCL students to do.) I had some general ideas that evolved over time, however, starting with wanting something bigger than Holladay, Utah.

I wanted to be well rounded, and have some meaningful relationships. I wanted to raise children who were well educated and self-reliant, with a solid work ethic and respect for all kinds of people. I knew I couldn't change the world but I wanted to contribute in some areas.

Financially, I wanted to have enough. I didn't aspire to be rich, but being able to pay the bills and having a degree of professional independence were important to me. My upbringing also had instilled a strong sense of responsibility to my family and the community.

I certainly wasn't counting on a large inheritance. I would be making my own way for the most part. I was pleasantly surprised by and grateful for the help my grandmother did provide over the years: financing for my first car, $20,000 during graduate school, and a $200,000 trust at her death in 1972.

My wealth goals have been quite consistent, although different ones have taken priority at different times in my life. (See the box on the next page.) My financial targets evolved as my wealth grew. Early on, I thought that making three times what my father did would be amazing. (He never made more than $25,000.)

---

26. The question is from a poem called "The Summer Day," by Mary Oliver.

> **HOWARD'S WEALTH GOALS**
>
> 1. Provide security for me and my dependent family.
> 2. Provide a base for the success of family members as they pursue their desired careers.
> 3. Help other people whom I know and care about, to address specific needs that can be met with money.
> 4. Serve the needs of society in areas that I find important, and where my contribution can have an impact.

My two-pronged strategy for building personal wealth was: (1) try to have a good job and supplement it with outside asset-building activities, and (2) live within my means, managing outflows so that my net worth would go up each year. I paid close attention to my bottom line.

I always had a paid job and worked at various things to build outside assets, including board work, real estate investing and some dabbling in the stock market. Investing—personal and professional—would prove to be the real growth engine, starting with Baupost.

I have always been disciplined about wealth planning. SFILP was designed to structure our total family holdings so that growth occurred in the pockets of the next generation while stable investments were kept in Fredi's and my hands. And, as I've said more than once, I work hard to minimize estate taxes.

I started estate planning early with an attitude that is somewhere between "You can't take it with you," and "*Après moi, le déluge.*" After I'm gone, it's someone else's problem but I have a responsibility to set up structures and help the people and causes that I care about.

The ultimate estate plan, some say, is to make sure that your check to the undertaker bounces. Fredi and I don't want to cut it that close or be in a position of having to ask our kids for help. However, each time our holdings exceed what we feel we need, we make gifts to our family and our communities.

If all that sounds like a lot of work, it is. There are lots of gray areas, like when does life insurance make sense? (I still struggle somewhat with that.) Also, you have to pay attention to the details without losing sight of the big picture.

I like to know where I stand, so I calculate my net worth every month, using a massive spreadsheet on my computer to get a 30,000 foot view. I also do a two-year cash flow, every two years. It has never worked out exactly as planned, but it allows me to see the possibilities based on available information.

How *has* it worked out, you ask?

Mindful of Wealth Management Principle 5—scorecards matter—I track personal net worth, household net worth, and total wealth for the family. We can't complain, as you can see from the almost four decades of results shown in **Figure 5-1**.

FIGURE 5-1
Building and Managing Wealth: Howard's Scorecard
(net worth—$ millions after tax)

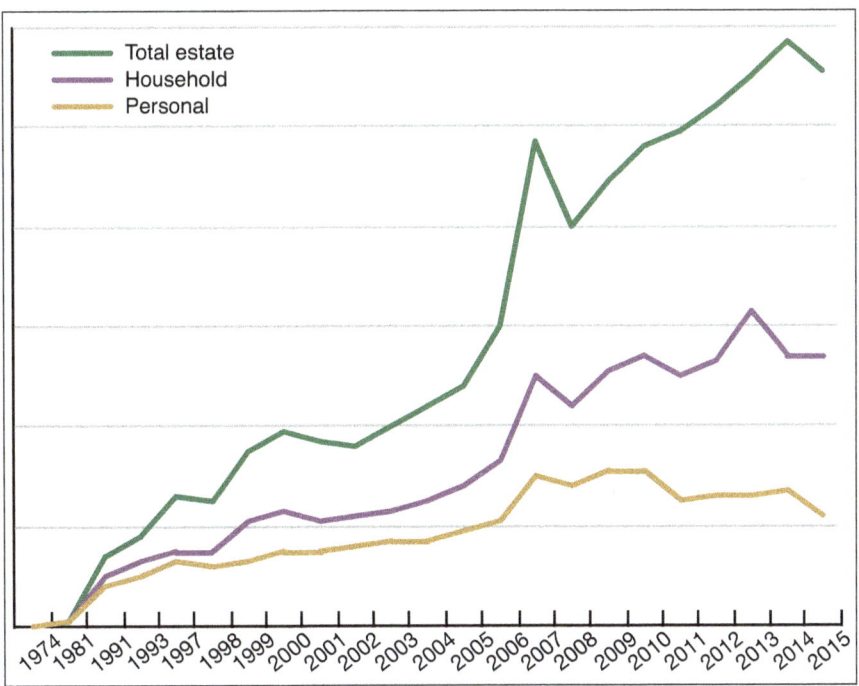

My scorecard reflects my wealth management strategies over the years and our good fortune as a family through the ups and downs of the market.

SFILP accounts for a large part of total wealth. Personal and household assets mainly consist of cash, loans, and some Baupost and pension investments. They also include my grandmother's trust and our charitable trust but their disposition is not in my estate.

The exact numbers for each metric matter less than the general trends. Perhaps even more interesting is what is missing from the chart; income taxes took away approximately 30% of assets, and gifts (to charity, family members and other individuals) another 14%.

Is my approach to wealth management right for everyone?

Probably not, but that's not the point. The point is that you need to figure out an approach that is right for *you*, and find whatever help you need to develop a good plan and execute it well. That's what being financially responsible means.

We'll be talking more about getting and using help in *Chapter 7*. But first, let's take a brief detour into the world of investing. Active investing has served me and my family well, but it's harder than a lot of what you hear and read would suggest.

It also may not be the right investment strategy for you. As more than one friend has pointed out to me, unless you have considerable time, talent, and interest for investing yourself, an S&P index fund is better and safer than trusting any paid advisor or trying to beat the market from home.

Still curious? Read on!

WHAT I THINK I KNOW ABOUT INVESTING

MY SUGGESTED TITLE for this chapter was "Confessions of a Successful Investor: I Really Didn't Know What I Was Doing!" Investing is a complicated endeavor, as I've learned over the years by observing, reading, asking a lot of questions . . . and trial and error.

We'll start there, with my investing education. I'll then offer my perspectives on investing, illustrated by how we have applied them in the Stevenson family partnership and what we have learned from that experience.

MY INVESTING EDUCATION

MY INTEREST IN investing began in my late teens, when I heard about stocks and became fascinated by them. Holladay, Utah, wasn't exactly a financial Mecca, but I learned what I could by reading the *Salt Lake Tribune*.

As an MBA student at HBS, I took a course in investing from George Bates. I learned about security markets, and Graham and Dodd's principles of value investing. After I got a teaching job, I began to do a little stock investing of my own. Some days, I was ahead; some days, behind.

My philosophy started to turn from public to private markets. You heard good stories from Goldman Sachs and others but I couldn't distinguish among them. My information was limited and I lost faith in my ability to predict. I tried to find good fund managers and wouldn't check the stock prices too often.

It made more sense to me to invest in companies that I was close to, often by serving on boards. Wolfe Industries was one of my first and most successful involvements, starting in 1973 and extending over decades. I charged them $300 a day for my board services and got 1% of stock.

I tagged along as Wolfe evolved from a lumber business in Ohio to nursing homes to Health Care & Retirement Corporation of America to Arbor Health Care. I made my first million dollars that way, and gained some lifelong friends and investment buddies including Pier Borra, Tom James and Fritz Wolfe.

My next investing experiment was real estate, where I learned from my South End Boston rehab experience that I don't like leverage. (I watched some friends go from rich to poor almost overnight.) Over time, I would come to see that leverage is fine, as long as it is constrained to the deal.

When I started the entrepreneurship program at HBS, I decided that I needed to know more about venture capital. I saw capital market myopia[27] and learned that investing was a fashion business. Some seasons, venture capital was a good bet. Other times, real estate or the stock market were the stars. Some deals didn't seem to make sense but worked out; others looked great, then fizzled.

I came to believe that it wasn't good to be wedded to any particular style of investing. My basic skepticism that you can't predict the future was strongly reinforced.

I got my first taste as a professional investor when I went to work with Matt Simmons in 1970. We raised debt and equity, and were doing early stage leveraged buyouts (LBOs) before anyone knew what the words were. My years at Baupost built on all that experience (except the LBOs). It's a story worth telling in some detail.

The story begins with Bill Poorvu, the Harvard School of Design professor I recruited to help teach real estate at HBS. Bill also was one of

---

27. Bill Sahlman and I have a chapter called "Capital Market Myopia" in *Venture Capital*, Edward Elgar Publishing Ltd., 2003.

the founders and owners of WCVB-TV, Channel 5 in Boston. In the mid-1970s, the station's leadership came under pressure from shareholders to sell.

Bill wanted more time and asked me for help. I taught him about leveraged recaps, which allowed them to sell the station five years later for double what it would have got in 1978. Bill and a few of the other sellers decided to keep their money together and start an investment firm. Would I join them?

I didn't know where it would lead but it was a unique opportunity. I was in, with 150% at risk.

We started in January 1982 with $27 million in assets. We spoke to 40 to 50 people, to get an understanding of the industry. We heard the same story over and over, which wasn't very satisfying. How could you make money if everyone was investing in recreational vehicles?

That winter, Bill identified Seth Klarman, one of his students, as a star. Together, we began to develop an investment philosophy hallmarked by a very strong value discipline. Because we were handling all of our various clients' money, we didn't want to limit ourselves just to stocks. We looked for value wherever we could find it.

We also decided that Baupost employees—including me—would invest all of our money in the partnership, on the same terms as client investors. That, we figured, was the best way to ensure a true alignment of interests.

In May, Seth joined Baupost on a full-time basis. We began looking for opportunities.

We were wary of the herd mentality. We were patient, willing to sit on cash and wait for the right opportunity. We also would sell early, to reduce risk. The saying still goes that "the best time to buy is when Baupost sells."

Seth and I recruited people who liked to scout for value stocks and other deep value securities. We would cast a wide net and quickly zero in. We were a bit ahead of the game, looking at things like distressed debt, and we were creative (e.g., investing $100 in each of 2500 mutual savings banks).[28]

Baupost was quickly outperforming everybody, and today ranks among the top ten hedge funds in size ($29 billion) and long-term returns

---

28. We became a depositor when the banks converted to a regular corporation. In that way, we invested and got equity plus the existing surplus.

(16% per year net to investors, with only three negative years). Seth has proved to be a genius at investing over the last 33 years.

Starting Baupost in 1982, at the absolute nadir of the market, was great timing. But I attribute a lot of the success to its value discipline and lack of constraints. I resigned as general partner in 1991, but I continue to serve as co-chair of Baupost's Advisory Board.

Bessemer Securities was another tremendous learning opportunity for me. My involvement there began in 1996, as a board member and co-investor. I got to see world-class money managers at work.

Bessemer's company investment strategy was to make a large number of small bets. A high percentage became write-offs but the winners far outstripped the losers. It earned spectacular returns over the 1998–2001 period by riding the Internet and communications wave.

Despite those positive experiences—in part, because of them—I continue to harbor a healthy skepticism about the investment profession. One big problem, in my view, is that modern portfolio theory still underlies most of what professional investment firms and consultants in the field sell.

Modern finance theory essentially is a mathematical formulation of the concept of diversification. Harry Markowitz launched the revolution in 1952. The increasing computer power available to support its statistical approach to investing has helped it flourish.

My basic objection to modern portfolio theory is that statistical models do not match the real world. They also are easy to misuse, a problem that the mathematician Daniel Ellenberg's recent book calls "statistical bamboozlement and deceit."[29]

I could go on, but I won't. Others have written more compellingly than I can about some of the warning flags, including Michael Lewis (*Flash Boys* and *The Big Short*), Nate Silver (*The Signal and the Noise*) and Simon Lack (*The Hedge Fund Mirage*).

Instead—perhaps even better—we will offer a funny but sobering cartoon that was so popular during the bear market of 2008 that it inspired its creator, Scott Adams, to write an equally entertaining blog called "Markets Explained."[30]

---

29. *How Not to Be Wrong: The Power of Mathematical Thinking*, Jordan Ellenberg, The Penguin Press, 2014.
30. You can find the blog at *http://dilbert.com/blog/entry/financial_markets_explained/*.

DILBERT © 2008 Scott Adams. Used By permission of UNIVERSAL UCLICK. All rights reserved.

MY PERSPECTIVES ON INVESTING

ACCORDING TO BRITANNICA, lotteries, organized football (soccer) pools, horse racing, casinos and poker are today's most popular gambling activities. And, they add, insurance and stock markets also are forms of gambling in the broadest sense. Sounds right to me.

Some of you may remember a Kenny Rogers song called "The Gambler." (See the box below.) It offers words of wisdom for investors as well as poker players. We will be saying much the same thing but his song is more memorable.

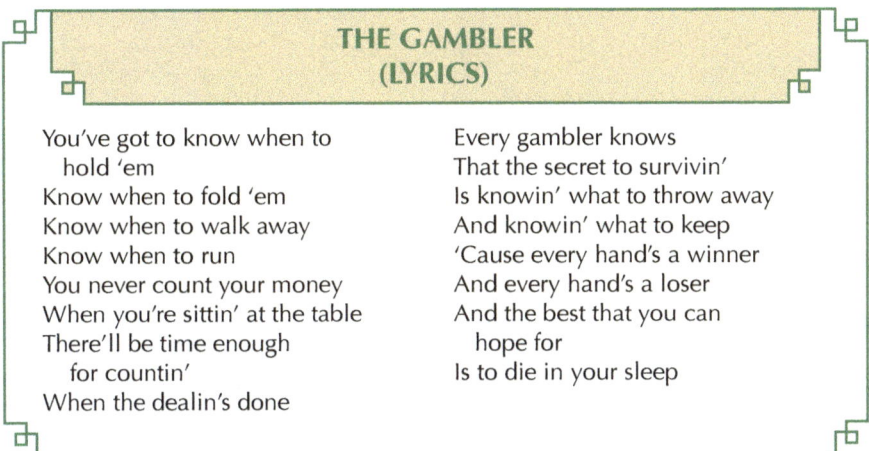

THE GAMBLER (LYRICS)

You've got to know when to hold 'em
Know when to fold 'em
Know when to walk away
Know when to run
You never count your money
When you're sittin' at the table
There'll be time enough
for countin'
When the dealin's done

Every gambler knows
That the secret to survivin'
Is knowin' what to throw away
And knowin' what to keep
'Cause every hand's a winner
And every hand's a loser
And the best that you can
hope for
Is to die in your sleep

Perhaps not surprisingly, I also see a strong parallel between entrepreneurship and investing.

Investing and entrepreneurship are both about pursuing *opportunities* through *deals* with other *people* in always changing *contexts*. An investor who has accumulated resources can diversify his investments, but the mechanics for any given bet are the same.

Now, how to go about the business of investing?

I have come up with some rules for investing based on my investing education and experience. (See the box below for the latest version.) They represent a philosophy of investing that is a balance between optimism and skepticism and—I like to think—is more realistic than most.

> ### HOWARD'S PRINCIPLES OF INVESTING
>
> 1. Think through your investment goals.
> 2. Be skeptical of investment "experts."
> 3. Avoid the herd or get trampled.
> 4. Don't measure yourself on short-term, relative performance.
> 5. Make sure you have real diversification.
> 6. Develop a rich deal stream.
> 7. Invest bottom up but check top down.
> 8. Figure out the payoff matrix and probabilities.
> 9. Know the rules before you decide to play.
> 10. Understand the real constraints.
> 11. Don't strive for perfect information.
> 12. Figure out what has to happen for you to win.
> 13. Understand the risks you are taking.
> 14. "Rightsize" your bets.
> 15. Pick an A person with a B idea over a B person with an A idea.
> 16. Run from any sign of dishonesty.
> 17. Remember that everyone wants something from a deal.
> 18. Weigh participant costs against potential benefits.
> 19. Ask your question even if you think it's stupid.
> 20. Read the deal documents carefully.
> 21. Focus on when to get out.
> 22. Don't expect to maximize total returns.
> 23. Be disciplined about valuations.
> 24. Don't cheat at solitaire.

Like Moses' Ten Commandments, my investing rules are clear enough but can be hard to follow, with all sorts of contradictions and definitional issues. Our family partnership experience confirms that reality while also demonstrating that using the principles—in our case at least—can have positive results.

A CASE STUDY: SFILP

I SET UP the Stevenson Family Investment Limited Partnership in 1993 as a device for building and leveraging scale among our family's investment activities. I think of it as a family service and resist calling it a family office. (We will never offer concierge services.)

SFILP has been an experiment in active investing at a relatively small scale, using my investing principles and continuously learning through trial and error.

Our primary goal is to produce long-term steady growth. We are value investors, looking for opportunities wherever we can find them. We are conservative investors, looking for bets with considerable upside while protecting ourselves from having to sell at the wrong time.

Successful implementation requires true diversification, access to deal streams, and the discipline to flexibly follow our principles. Our portfolio structure, which reflects our attention to upside potential and downside risk, has three broad types of investments, each playing a distinct role:

- *Anchor investments* provide a low downside with a nice upside. (Baupost has served us well in that category and we hold cash.)

- *Opportunity investments* offer some upside with a downside that we believe will never go to zero. (We rely on public securities funds, each of which uses a different strategy to reduce risk.)

- *Opportunistic investments* have the potential for a meaningful upside without damaging the portfolio. All can go to zero so we aim for a lot of shots on goal, and focus on early stage and expanding ventures without many startups.

We take a somewhat idiosyncratic approach to placing bets, reflecting what we have to work with in terms of time, talent and resources.

We don't have swarms of analysts for due diligence, but have developed a quick and dirty approach for vetting private deals that focuses on identifying the key drivers. We still aren't a big fish in the investing pond, but have built extensive networks for accessing and partnering on deals.

We are patient investors, looking for long-term success. Our best investments took over ten years to come to fruition, sometimes with perks (e.g., dividends) along the way. In the meantime, we were gaining tax efficiencies by not turning over deals.

You have to pay attention, though, along the way. Investing is a dynamic, unpredictable game. The initial bet is just the start of what usually is a series of decisions about adding or taking out money. Each is a decision impacting your investment return. The bet may have changed for any number of reasons.

It's easy to kid yourself, though.

Doing well? It's tempting to ride the momentum but almost always dangerous. Losing money? Putting in "just a few more dollars" often is unwise. Being very clear about what you're betting on will help you know whether you have won or lost, and decide whether and when to get out.

You also need to be careful not to forget this rightsizing rule: Don't let anything get too big. SFILP is somewhat unique, we believe, in that one of our core disciplines is to take some money off the table when we have the opportunity.

Now the big question: How are we doing? The short answer is that the experiment seems to be working, so far.

Over its lifetime, SFILP has returned over 16.5% pretax, which is 33 times the money invested and well ahead of the S&P's 6.6% growth for that time frame. Our most recent ten-year returns were 18% and our fifteen-year returns 13%, compared to 4.9% and 2.1% respectively for the S&P.

Those figures are averages, of course, and mask a lot of SFILP activity, a wide range of bets, and mixed results.

Our SFILP database has almost 1,500 lines, each representing a transaction[31] across hundreds of entities. Our individual investments ranged from a $10,000 play to a million dollar bet. Results ranged from negative numbers to over 400 times our investment.

Of the entities, the majority were individual deals in private companies, including search fund "finds" and co-investments with Bessemer. They included our biggest hits but also racked up some total losses. Our pooled funds generally (and as expected) produced more middle-of-the-road results.

What makes for a winner or a loser?

Early in my investing career, I tried all sorts of analyses, searching for some useful patterns. Sector? Timing? Geography? Deal type? Deal source?

---

31. A transaction is any time we put money into or take money out of a company or fund.

None emerged as significant. I shook my head, and reminded myself: You can't predict the outcome.

Recently, as Andy and I reminisced about the deals we've done, a set of categories emerged that describes our experience in psychological terms. Each deal fell somewhere along a spectrum: stuff happens, wrong on the bet, made it safely, pleasant surprise, or WOW (Wondrous Occasional Win).

Our analysis showed that we were wrong on the bet or a victim of circumstance over half of the time. Ouch. Fortunately, those experiences were more than offset by pleasant surprises. The real secret to our success, however, was a tiny sliver of hits in the WOW category.

Closer analysis didn't solve that pesky prediction problem but did offer a few insights. For one, getting some money back regardless of the category is important. For another, context, opportunity, deal and people all are important, but people will make it or break it for you.

It's also worth noting that there's a difference between performance and results. I have a formula for that: *Effort + Skill = Performance; Performance + Luck = Results.* We try to allocate our efforts wisely, we hope that we demonstrate skill, and we know that we've had some exceptional luck.

At the end of the day, investing is a humbling experience.

Perhaps our strength with SFILP is knowing that we can't predict the future, and that often it's better to be lucky than smart. SFILP also has the benefit of people we trust—family members with their own money at stake—running it.

Now, let's delve into the challenges of getting and using help, in the next chapter.

GETTING AND USING PROFESSIONAL HELP

I HAVE BENEFITED tremendously from all kinds of help during my wealth journey.

Some help has been personal and informal. My sons participate in managing our family investment partnership. Friends and trusted advisors are invaluable sounding boards, and occasionally serve as trustees for our family trusts. My professional network provides access to investment information and deals.

It's almost impossible to accumulate wealth of any significance, however, without professional help. In the early stages, it may be a financial planner[32] and a tax accountant. As you move along the wealth spectrum, it gets increasingly complicated.

My experience has left me with what I consider to be a healthy respect for *and* skepticism towards wealth professionals. Most of all, it has reinforced my belief that anyone who tries to take away your sense of responsibility for your financial future is not doing you any favors.

This chapter aims to help you be an educated client.

As background, we'll start with a brief look at the wealth management industry and its offerings, including financial education. We'll then explore some broad questions that you need to ask yourself, to be a proactive and confident user of the vast array of services available.

---

32. Kathy Kristoff offers some useful guidance on hiring financial planners in *Investing 101* (see Chapter 16), Bloomberg Press, 2009.

THE WEALTH MANAGEMENT INDUSTRY

WEALTH MANAGEMENT IS big business. Boston Consulting Group estimates that global private wealth grew by 14.6% in 2013 to reach a total of $152 trillion, with North America accounting for $50.3 trillion. The gains reflect the improved performance of equity markets and the creation of new wealth.[33]

The industry faces lots of challenges, however. The wealthy continue to seek professional help but with less trust than before the financial crisis, and with an increased focus on transparency and risk. Business models are shifting as traditional channels compete and digital technology reshapes service delivery.

Who is considered a "wealthy" client? Financial service providers segment the market into five categories with increasingly sophisticated (and expensive) needs and wants. (See **Table 7-1**.)

TABLE 7-1
Wealth Market Segments

Category	Investible Assets
Mass affluent	$100,000–$1 million
High net worth	$1 million–$5 million
Very high net worth	$5 million–$30 million
Ultra-high net worth	$30 million+
Family offices	$100 million+

There are a myriad of people out there waiting to make money from your money. They can range from independent advisors to small firms to full-service financial supermarkets. Depending on where you fall on the wealth spectrum, different financial channels will be vying for your business.

For example, retail banks and online brokerages serve mass affluent individuals; registered investment advisors (RIAs) and full-service brokers move up the scale to high net worth clients; and pure private banks extend to ultra-high net worth individuals and family offices.

You also may need or want the help of lawyers, accountants, life insurers and other professionals. **Table 7-2** offers an illustrative array of service

---

33. *Global Wealth 2014: Riding a Wave of Growth*, Boston Consulting Group, June 9, 2014.

TABLE 7-2
Wealth Management Service Providers (Illustrative)

Provider	Services	Cost	Stated Objectives	Hidden Objectives?
Financial advisor	Investment strategy Portfolio management Money manager selection	Flat fee and/or commission	Provide perspective Achieve your goals	Create dependency CMA (Cover My Assets) and EYA (Expose Your Assets)
Investment manager	Pick securities	% of assets Performance fee	Beat market in assigned segment	Add client assets Avoid bottom quartile performance
Broker	Make the trade (intermediary)	Transaction-based fee	Good execution Good advice	Keep client Maximize fees
Outsourced CIO	Choose investment professionals	Asset-based fee	Give you access to and monitor money managers	Build asset base of their organization
Family wealth counselor	Give unbiased advice on family dynamics and governance	Fee	Effective family culture, governance, succession	Make parents feel in control
Multifamily office	Integrated wealth management	Fee or profit center	Coordinate all aspects of your family finances	Build asset base of their organization and keep client
Life insurer	Provide death benefits	Fees set by underwriters	Provide financial security for your family	Sell policies Earn interest on your premiums Hope for lapsed coverage
Lawyer	Strategic thinking Prepare/review documents	Hourly fee Some transaction-based fees	Protect you against risk Document what you want	Keep client Be indispensable Maximize billable hours
Accountant	Tax/other accounting Record keeping	Hourly fee	Tax knowledge Accurate reporting	Keep client Control critical documents

Note: Trustee services (which may be fulfilled by a lawyer or accountant) are discussed in Chapter 5.

providers, based on my experiences and my observations about their stated and (in my somewhat skeptical view)sometimes hidden objectives.[34]

FINANCIAL EDUCATION

THE RECENT ECONOMIC downturn raised awareness about the complexity of the financial marketplace and how ill-equipped many people are to make financial decisions. You don't need an MBA but you do need the basic financial skills and knowledge to make informed judgments and take effective action.

Fortunately (and sometimes unfortunately), that problem has spawned a variety of resources to help you strengthen your financial IQ.

At last look, Amazon offered 101,705 books on personal finance. Its list of 6,392 wealth management titles was led by *Wealth Management Unwrapped*, which urges readers to be CEOs of their own wealth and learn how to work effectively with their advisors.[35]

There are magazines dedicated to personal finance too, and many newspapers offer regular columns and special features on the subject. Financial service firms offer information (e.g., Northern Trust's *Wealth* magazine with its "financial and lifestyle perspective") and seminars and programs abound.

One book that I have recommended to friends and family is *Wealth: Grow It and Protect It* by Stuart E. Lucas.[36]

Stuart is a fourth-generation heir of the Carnation Company founder, and the chairman of Wealth Strategist Partners, which offers investment advisory and strategic consulting services to very wealthy individuals and families. He also teaches at the University of Chicago's Booth School of Business.

Booth's four-day Private Wealth Management (PWM) program attracts first-generation entrepreneurs, multigenerational inheritors, family business owners, and purely financial families from around the world. They often come with spouses, children and extended families.

The Wharton School of Business has gone a step further, establishing a Wealth Management Initiative that conducts research, offers educational

---

34. A word of caution: Job titles and roles are somewhat fuzzy in the financial services sector; a broker also may be referred to as a financial advisor, for example.
35. *Wealth Management Unwrapped* (Rosetta Books, 2014) was written by Charlotte B. Beyer, a Wall Street veteran and the founder of the Institute for Private Investors (IPI).
36. *Wealth: Grow It and Protect It*, Stuart E. Lucas, FT Press, 2012.

programming (including private wealth management), and partners with organizations to create conferences and publications about financial industry issues.

However you attain it, financial education can and should help you better understand and navigate the murky waters of wealth management services. It also, if you happen to be a parent, can help you be a more effective teacher and role model for your kids. (More on that in *Chapter 10.*)

GETTING AND USING THE RIGHT HELP

YOU NEED TO be an informed, proactive, thoughtful and—yes—skeptical client. **Figure 7-1** summarizes the three questions that you must ask and answer to find and effectively use the right wealth management services.

FIGURE 7-1
Wealth Management Services: Three Questions

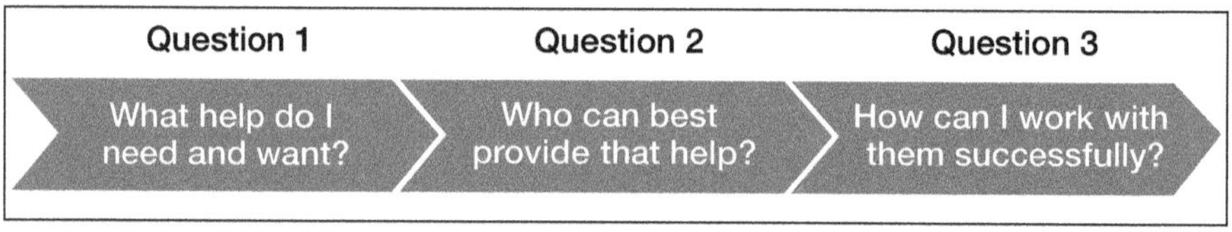

Question 1	Question 2	Question 3
What help do I need and want?	Who can best provide that help?	How can I work with them successfully?

Question 1—What Help Do I Need and Want?

A NUMBER OF factors should be considered as you assess your requirements including your wealth management goals, your attitudes about wealth and investing, your knowledge and skills, your desire for control, and the amount of time and money you have available. (See **Table 7-3**.)

These factors collectively will influence your wealth management and investment strategies which, in turn, will determine your service needs. For example, buying an index fund is much different from active investing.

The other big question, of course, is whether to outsource the work at all. Are you able and willing to do it yourself?

When we decided that SFILP needed more than our nights-and-weekend attention, we solicited proposals from three firms: a major trust company, a financial firm used by HBS to counsel faculty members, and a financial and tax management firm founded by a venture capital acquaintance.

We were somewhat appalled at the costs, and not certain that we needed or wanted some of the services bundled in with basic investment

TABLE 7-3
Assessing Your Needs and Preferences

Factor	Questions to Ask Yourself
Goals	What are my wealth management priorities: accumulation, capital preservation, wealth transfer, philanthropy or spending power?
Attitudes	How interested am I in money matters? How do I feel about investing? How important is tax efficiency to me? What is my tolerance for risk? For complexity?
Knowledge and skills	How strong are my wealth management abilities? Do I have the network and skills needed for investing?

management. We were glad when Andy—who fortunately had the skills and interest—agreed to take on full-time management of the partnership.

Finally, it's important to appreciate that this will not be a one-time exercise. Your goals, strategies and service requirements will change along with your personal and financial circumstances, and likely will be quite different at ages 20, 40 and 60.

For now, we'll assume that you have determined your needs and wants. On to the next challenge: How to decide—first among the various provider types, and then among the many individuals and firms offering those types of services?

Question 2—Who Can Best Provide That Help?

THE KEY QUESTION for any service provider is: What services will I get, at what cost? Understanding the rules of the game will be critical, to answer those questions. Then it comes down to the people: Can I trust them with my money?

The list of service providers shown in **Table 7-2** can be broadly divided into three categories: wealth managers, money managers, and other professionals (lawyers, etc.). Each category will have some distinctive characteristics but also include some quite different kinds of players.

To illustrate, let's take a closer look at the two categories most deeply involved in your financial affairs: wealth managers (including wealth advisors and multifamily offices) and money managers (including traditional investment managers and hedge fund/private equity firms).

Wealth Managers

Wealth managers essentially are stewards of your assets, with a fiduciary responsibility to act in the best interests of their clients.

Wealth advisors develop customized financial plans and investment policies, make investing recommendations, monitor performance, and handle administration. They may be affiliated with a financial institution or operate independently. They usually are supported by an administrative team, and sometimes by an investment professional.

It's a complicated job.

A successful wealth advisory team managing $10 million to $50 million in assets per client may have 30 clients. Each client typically will have three "pots" of money (taxable, tax-deferred, tax-exempt) and often more (trusts, children's accounts) for a total of 90 or more pots per advisor.

If the advisor makes 10 recommendations to buy or sell an investment within each pot each year, that will come to 900 investment decisions made for or with their clients annually. Then there are tax, estate planning, cash flow management, life insurance, banking and other financial needs to be addressed.

A wealth advisory team may make a few million dollars in revenue from fees that vary depending on the asset base size (e.g., 100 basis points to start and 20 to 40 points at $100 million). However, they also may be getting commissions or brokerage fees from financial services they recommend. (You need to ask.)

A *multifamily office* offers scale, skills and infrastructure that most individual families don't have. Integration of wealth planning (e.g., financial, philanthropic) and administrative management are core services. Most offices also offer family governance support (e.g., family meetings).

Some offices also offer family business services, personal financial education and planning for individual family members, and concierge services (e.g., travel planning). They generally make their money from asset-based fees, providing the other services "for free."

Money Managers

Money managers are investment professionals who build and manage portfolios of securities on behalf of clients. They do not have a fiduciary responsibility. They are only required to ensure that an investment is suitable for a client, which can create a potential conflict of interest.

A *traditional investment management* firm can earn a respectable living by charging 6 to 8 basis points for managing EFTs (Exchange Traded Funds) or a Standard & Poor index fund. They charge a substantially higher fee for active management (i.e., buying and selling specific investments within a portfolio).

The world of a *hedge fund or private equity* manager is entirely different. They can earn billions of dollars in a good year, in no small part thanks to a compensation system that is usually presented as standard market terms: the 2 + 20 formula.

I can't resist using the 2 + 20 formula as an example of how costs may be a real constraint or a phony constraint, can lead to unintended behaviors on the part of your friendly money manager, and are a real drain on your wealth. Here goes!

With 2 + 20 terms, the money manager gets 2% of total asset value as a fixed management fee plus 20% of profits. The formula is meant to encourage alignment but the math favors the house and can cost you dearly. Here's how it can play out.

With no meaningful claw backs or high water marks,[37] a 25% gain year, followed by a 20% loss year, followed by a 25% gain year, followed by a 20% loss year can result in a loss of 7.7% for an investor but four great years for the money manager.

If the loss years are 25%, the investor loses over 18.9% of his money, even though the ups and downs were the same percentage. Even worse, the manager may slip in that you pay all deal expenses, to boot. (I've challenged more than one manager on that.)

Each part of the 2 + 20 formula has its problems.

Profit sharing makes sense at first blush. It should motivate fund managers to do their best, right? Unfortunately, it can create perverse incentives. Here are a few examples, all of which make the alignment of Limited Partner (LP) and General Partner (GP) interests problematic:

♦ When things are going well, it can create incentives under certain contracts to realize the gains. This is particularly true if the fund is entering a fund-raising cycle.

♦ Under other contracts, fees are paid without realizing the "profit" so that temporary gains transfer wealth from LPs to GPs.

---

37. Hurdles, claw backs and high water marks are mechanisms for taking into account that the path to long run returns is rarely a straight line.

- There is an incentive to extend the partnership, so the GP will come into the performance fee.

- There are incentives to bet the ranch at the end of a losing fund.

The fixed fee is meant to cover fund management costs and usually is calculated as a percentage of assets under management. As funds and firms grow large, the fixed fees become a very lucrative part of the deal, hence the desire not to lose assets and the desperate attempts to hang onto clients.

Performance fees are another source of revenue for GPs. At Baupost, in the early years, we only charged performance fees when pretax returns exceeded the one-year Treasury bill rate compounded for five years. It still does not charge the so-called standard fee.

These days, I believe that 12% is the right target for pretax return prospects.

At 12%, the winnings are split approximately two-thirds to LPs and one-third to GPs, which seems almost fair to me. At lower than 12% market return, the split isn't fair and it's extremely hard to find funds that you truly believe will deliver more than 12% on a sustained basis.[38]

If you are making a large enough investment to have some bargaining power, deal terms like 2 + 20 likely can be renegotiated. Still, it is not a level playing field. It pays to understand the rules, assess whether you can work them to your advantage, and then decide whether you want to play.

The People Factor

Professional services are, well, professional services. You essentially are betting on the integrity, talent and luck of the people you hire to help you, even if they are using fancy financial models.

At SFILP, we have developed some criteria that I think generally apply to all wealth management service providers, in the following order of importance:

- *Ethical*—You try to determine that by understanding what they do in some depth. In truth, however, you can never fully protect yourself from a Madoff.

---

38. Certainly projections by experts like PIMCO and Grantham, Mayo, and van Otterloo don't forecast such high returns over the intermediate term.

- *Curious*—They have to be looking over the horizon, always on the watch for changes.

- *Smart*—The tricky thing here is that skill and results are not always correlated; luck can win over skill in the short run.

- *Experienced*—Generally, more is better and we're leery of someone who claims to never have had a bad experience. (If true, they have lost an opportunity to learn.)

- *Decent track records*—Even the best rarely can stay in the top investment quartile consistently. We're happy with people who remain in the upper half, year in and year out.

- *Transparent*—We look for sensible analytics, and honesty about both the good and the bad.

Okay, you're sold. You've done your due diligence—credentials checked, costs dissected, key people interviewed. You've read the contract carefully (Don't forget that part!) and signed on the dotted line. Now . . . .

Question 3—How Can I Work with Them Successfully?

The answer to this question will partly depend on whether the services being provided are episodic in nature or regular, ongoing activities. The latter will require more of an investment of your time and attention to build and maintain an effective working relationship.

Being clear on what kind of relationship you want—or don't want—with your advisor is important.

Do you want an active relationship or is a quarterly talk just fine? Do you expect what a friend of mine calls "entertainment value" or "brain candy," a steady flow of new ideas to talk about at cocktail parties? Do you care about wining and dining and golf outings? (Personally, I'd rather have my advisor working hard at managing my financial affairs.)

Over the long run, trust is important for a good relationship but accountability systems are even more important. Does the individual or firm managing your money have them in place? It's in everyone's best interest (but especially yours) to raise questions like this with your advisor:

- How will your performance be measured?
- How will my investments be tracked?
- What management reports will you provide?
- Can I get online access to information whenever I want?
- What checks and balances do you have in place?

It also is important to keep a keen eye on costs as well as performance. You have to continually monitor fees, expenses and tax efficiency, especially when wealth and investment professionals move into new fields as they inevitably will do.

Stuart offers a handy cost benchmark in an article called "The 50% Rule: Keep More Profits in Your Wallet."[39] Basically, he says that if you're giving up more than 50% of your profits to investment professionals and the government, you should reassess your approach.

Finally, I watch for any hint of dishonesty.

Obfuscating about fees or bragging about shark deals are bad signs. I saw a huge red flag when the first client communication from the new president of an investment firm was all about how profitable he was going to make the firm, with nary a mention of client service or results.

LAST WORDS: BUYER BEWARE

PROSPECTIVE CLIENTS HAVE to sit through a lot of sales pitches from so-called experts who are highly incented to get your business and build their revenues and profits. They have many tricks.

Selling to your fears is one. ("Risk averse? Tax phobic? We can fix that!") Another is to make everything seem complicated so they'll look smart. Or they will toss out an "As you know . . ." so you'll be embarrassed to admit that you don't understand.

The lesson is: Don't be fooled or intimidated by fast-talking professionals with lots of charts, technical jargon, and self-justification.

Here is a timeworn but useful saying: "There's no such thing as a stupid question." It is closely related to another one: "The least questioned

---

39. You can download a copy of "The 50% Rule" article at *http://wealthstrategistpartners.com/insights-and-news/*

assumption is often the most questionable." Asking questions can get to interesting discussions.

I'll sometimes say, "Help me understand. I'm not as smart as you." It forces a simple explanation. You may then discover that what they're saying is gobbledygook. The question can reveal some not readily apparent assumptions or misperceptions too, and may lead to creative thinking about alternatives.

We'll leave you with Scott Adam's wry take on the challenges of getting and using professional help. Then, on to Part III, Wealth and Families.

PART III

WEALTH & FAMILIES

OVER THE YEARS, I have been involved in many family wealth conferences, both as a speaker and as a participant. They often are billed like this: "A forum for sharing philosophies and practices of successful families in creating wealth in each generation, and managing the impact of wealth on family members."

Each time I hear that, I feel my thinly veiled cynicism surfacing. It's not that I think that what family wealth experts are selling is *bad*. I just don't think that it's *realistic*, especially as families become increasingly complex.[40]

One wealth expert that we interviewed readily conceded that there are overwhelming amounts of information and adrenalin out there, and not a lot of good education about the problem. I don't claim to have the perfect solution, but I am happy to share my experiences and conclusions.

We will start with my rebuttal to traditional family wealth models in *Chapter 8*. In *Chapter 9*, I will offer a family wealth philosophy based on my observations and (mal)practice. We will close with some lessons learned about raising wealthy kids in *Chapter 10*.

---

40. "U.S. Trust Survey Finds Modern American Family Dynamics Complicate Wealth Management," U.S. Trust, June 20, 2014 (*http://newsroom.bankofamerica.com/press-releases/us-trust/us-trust-survey-finds-modern-american-family-dynamics-complicate-wealth-management*).

A REBUTTAL TO FAMILY WEALTH MODELS

MOST MODELS FOR family wealth management hinge on what I have concluded to be three fallacies: (1) the possibility of achieving multigenerational wealth transfer, (2) an oversimplified definition of family, and (3) the value of top-down family governance. We'll tackle each one, in turn.

FALLACY 1—MULTIGENERATIONAL FAMILY WEALTH

FAMILY WEALTH PROFESSIONALS love to play to clients' shirtsleeves to shirtsleeves fears, the oft-cited phenomenon where the family business or family wealth dissipates over three generations.

A typical line is: "Research has found that 90% of inheritance is often depleted by the third generation." That is closely followed by: "Not necessarily true for you and yours, however; *you* can sustain your family forever!"

It's not that complicated, it seems. You pass down what you have amassed, equally by generation. And, you make sure there is at least one wealth generator in each generation to add what's required to make sure that everyone is taken care of, down the line.

That makes sense, right? No, not really. I must confess to a very basic problem with this model: God didn't hand me a pile of money and say, "Pass it down." But even if that were my goal, there are a lot of practical problems.

FIGURE 8-1 Spotlight on Great-Great-Grandfather Soffe

The first problem is simply keeping track of family.

It becomes nearly impossible to keep accurate family records due to the sheer number of people over time, multiple name changes through marriage, and the increasing geographic dispersion of family members.

I sometimes illustrate the proliferation problem using one branch of the Stevenson family tree that you saw in *Chapter 1*. I point to my great-great-grandfather, Nimrod George Soffe, who was born in 1826. He's the one with the impressive beard, circled at the bottom of the chart. (See **Figure 8-1**.)

In 1964, my father created a chart showing Nimrod's descendants. It's much too long to include here but I have unfurled it at some of the talks that I've given on family wealth. (Audience members seem impressed.)

The chart shows at least 483 descendants over 120 years, including 170 great-grandchildren (my father included). The number is probably understated; there are at least two people in the first generation after Nimrod for whom I can find no information.

Looking at the possibilities now, after 170 years, there could be some 4,000 to 8,000 living Nimrod Soffe descendants or at least people who could claim to be part of the extended family. (That range is based on two children per family per generation at the low end, and the Brady Bunch at the high end.)

The geographic dispersion problem became clear to me when I looked up Stevenson in the Arroyo Grande, California, phone book. (That's where my great-grandfather Stevenson died.) I found more than 30 listings. I'm sure that I am related to some of them but have no idea which ones, and I don't know what I would say if I called them.

The Dee lineage suffers from the same problems.

Grandpa Dee (#14 in **Figure 8-1**) had eight children. Family members worked hard to create a Dee family tree but with even a cursory examination, I could see that some people were missing and some names and locations were wrong. (Much of that family is still in Utah, but many have spread out.)

Now, the money problem. For the sake of argument, let's say that Nimrod's goal was for each grandchild to have the same wealth as he had, based solely on inheritance from him. The math doesn't look good.

To generate the same level of wealth for 8000 descendants, Nimrod's money would have to compound at approximately 5.5% steadily for 170 years starting at his birth. But you have to account for spending too. So the total actually would have to compound at 8.5%, assuming a pretax 3% spending rate.

The math gets even worse when you consider that our calculations don't account for income or inheritance taxes. Clearly, sustaining wealth across multiple generations through inheritance alone is a highly unlikely scenario, and the demands just get more unrealistic as family size grows.

(Of course, those calculations ignore the fact that there were 16 others who might have felt equal responsibility, and that there were marriages and divorces along the way that would contribute to and diminish the inheritance.)

For more sophisticated and skeptical audiences (yes, those HBS types), I beef up the analysis. I start with the observation that one dollar can't serve two purposes; wealth for the family's use has to come from somewhere.

Next, I offer a model used by a fifth generation family office to illustrate the problems of maintaining wealth. (See **Table 8-1**) The punch line is that if you try to live off income from capital—whether from a family business or investments—you have to do *really* well, or get the money elsewhere.

TABLE 8-1
Wealth for the Family's Use—A Model
(% of capital)

	From Family Business	From Family Investments
Spendable	2.4%	2.4%
Taxes	1.6%	1.6%
Dividend	4.0%	4.0%
Retained	4.0%	4.0%
Net	8.0%	8.0%
Tax	4.0%	N/A
Inflation	5.0%	5.0%
ROE Pretax*	17.0%	13.0%

*ROE = Return on equity

The real issue, however, is spending power for your parents, you, your heirs and beyond. The amount of wealth will make a difference but still, it's just a matter of time. If you have $1 billion, the game can last a while, but probably not at $100 million, and certainly not at $10 million.

Possible answers to the spending power problem include dropping your living standards or at least holding them steady; growing your business and/or investments faster; and getting an injection of entrepreneurial energy or outside wealth through hard work, marriage or other inheritances.

None of those solutions is a sure bet but I find the "wealth generator" concept the most suspect. How can you possibly know who—if anyone—not only will manage to generate the wealth but also will be happy to share it with everyone else in the family (most of whom they don't know)?

Now, let's dissect the notion of passing down your wealth equally by generation.

One problem is that family branches have different sizes, shapes and circumstances. The other is the presumption that "equal" and "fair" are the same thing. Here are just a few of the many dilemmas:

- ◆ Is it equal when one branch gets the same as another branch but there are more people in it to split the wealth?
- ◆ Is it equal when one person inherits when they are 25 but an older stepbrother doesn't get the money until he is 45?
- ◆ Is it fair when one person starts a firm that is wildly successful and another devotes himself to public school teaching?
- ◆ Is it fair when one family has a severely handicapped child to raise and support for the rest of her life?

The reality is that an equal division of money by generation will not translate to equal shares by person over time. As shown in **Figure 8-2,** there may be an 80 times difference in share of wealth at the fifth generation, de-

FIGURE 8-2
The Generation Gap

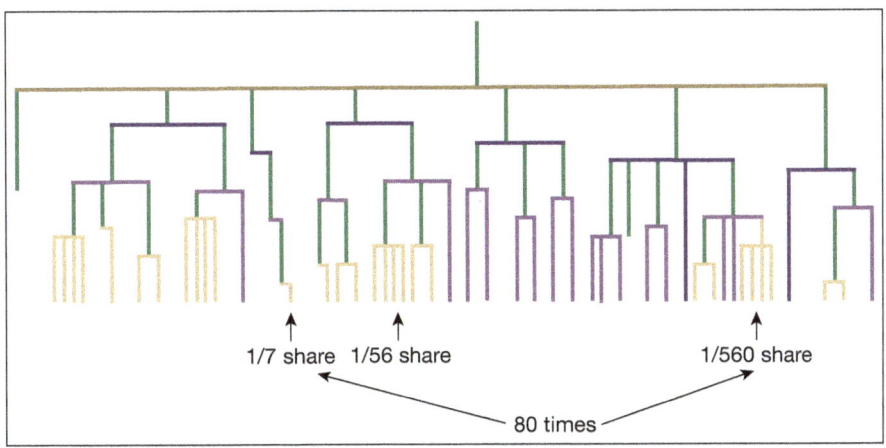

pending on where you sit. Even by the third generation, the difference may be fivefold.

The basic notion of generation is problematic too. On my latest family tree, some branches are at the ninth generation and others at the fifth. One of my grandchildren is now 24 years old while another is just past the four year mark. Same generation and same time frame but very different needs.

Other real-world complexities challenge the idea that you can control financial equality. What about the spouses' wealth; is marrying rich a plus or a minus? What about lifestyle choices? People spend their money differently, and that includes their inheritances.

My grandmother's trust, which she set up in 1962, is a good example of the last point. (See **Figure 8-3**.)

FIGURE 8-3
A Real Example: 50 Years in a Trust

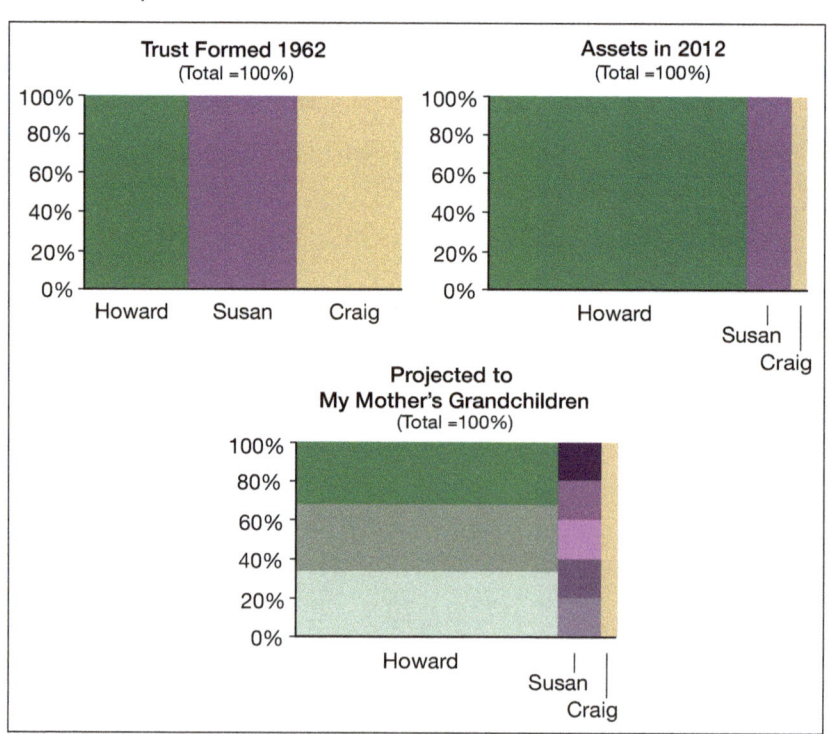

Her trust passed to my mother and then was divided equally among my brother, my sister and me on my mother's death in 1992. By 2012, that distribution had shifted dramatically even though all the assets were managed in a pool.

How did that happen? I can explain.

My brother was a big spender. I left my share untouched and watched it grow 55 times over 40 years. My sister falls somewhere in between. Our families vary in size too, resulting in big differences in the projected amounts for the grandchildren in each branch.

FALLACY 2—
DEFINITION OF FAMILY

I SEEM MORE confused than most on this subject. How *do* you define family?

The answer you often get is that it's about consanguinity, which is just a fancy term for being descended from the same ancestor as another person. There are even charts for determining degrees of relationship between, for example, third cousins thrice removed.

Consanguinity doesn't tell you much about the real relationship, however, and gets farcical after a while. My kids have half my genes and my grandchildren have one-fourth. At what point does it get so diluted that it is insignificant?

The emphasis on bloodlines may have made sense in the days when you grew up in one place, married someone from the next village, and lived out your days within a stone's throw. You knew everyone in your extended family, and your lives were intertwined.

That's still the case in some remote parts of the world but, for most of us, the world has become much more far-reaching and fluid. I wouldn't recognize most of my cousins if I ran into them. Some of my children and grandchildren are nearby, but some live across the country and some on another continent.

Now, let's talk about family trees.

Most family wealth experts take a hierarchical, top-down approach to drawing them, as illustrated in **Figure 8-4** on the next page. That, I would argue, is the wrong way to think about it.

The problem with this view is that it's all about *MY* family. In reality, my children, grandchildren and great-grandchildren also are part of other families with whole constellations of relatives. I have no more claim on them than two, four, eight or 16 other people.

FIGURE 8-4
Drawing the Family Tree—
The Wrong Way

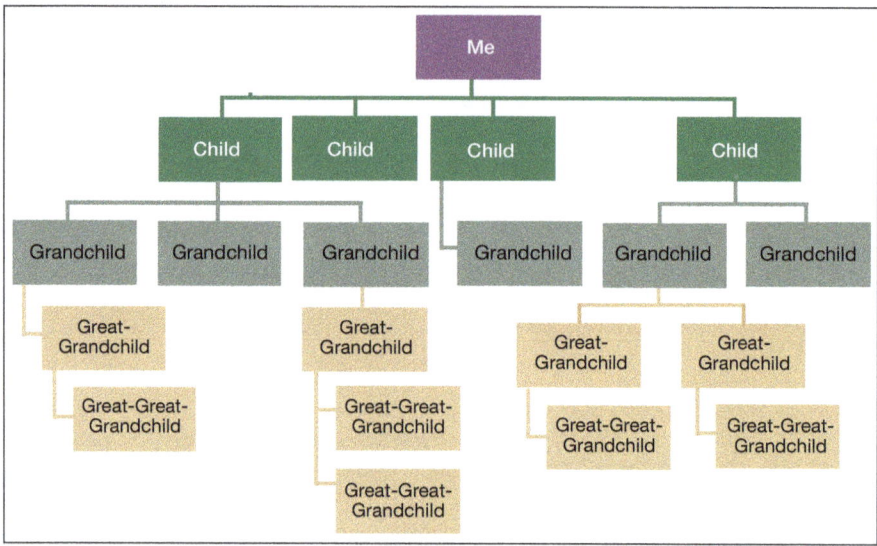

I actually find it more useful to flip the chart upside down, to see where you came from. (See **Figure 8-5**.) In my case, I inherited ideas and values from three grandparents whom I knew, two parents, and four uncles and aunts. Other family members dropped ideas in my head.

FIGURE 8-5
Drawing the Family Tree—
The Right Way

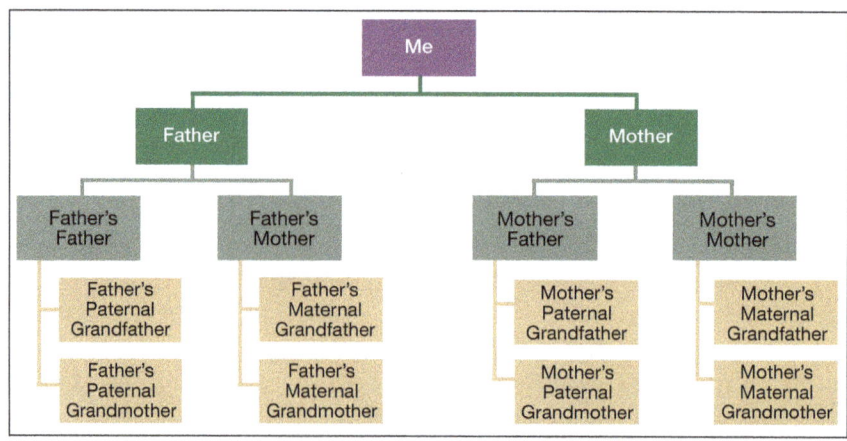

Arguably though, both chart styles are wrong (although the second is more useful). I actually view families as networked—not as hierarchical—organizations.

In networks, you form links with trusted individuals. When you need advice or support, you know who to reach out to, and you can be confident that he or she will be happy to help. I hope that is how our family operates.

Another problem is what is *not* shown in consanguinity tables and on many family trees. They may leave out individuals whom you care about and regard as family, even if they're not from the same gene pool. More dilemmas:

- Someone I know has excluded his adopted children from his estate. (I don't know if that's legal in all states, let alone moral.)
- How about family by marriage? (I can't imagine not helping my stepchildren.)
- What about illegitimate children? (They have the same percentage of your genes as your legitimate children, and what about taking responsibility for your actions?)

Finally, there is the essential question: For whom will you take responsibility? Defining family responsibilities is both a philosophical and a pragmatic question. You can set rules for who's in and who's out but that still leaves lots of questions about who is responsible for what.

My experience with my brother offers one example.

My brother was a lot smart and a little crazy. He skipped senior year of high school, and completed college in three and a half years along with naval ROTC. He graduated and was married the same day, and then went off to the Marines.

He became a major in the Naval Security Group, controlling overflights in Russia in the Gary Powers era[41] when there were lots of "training accidents." It was stressful work, and alcohol is a time-honored coping mechanism in the military. He developed a drinking problem.

My brother and his wife (who had a drug problem) adopted a child while they were stationed in Germany, and a second one when they re-

---

41. Gary Powers was an American military pilot whose spy plane was shot down over Russia in 1960.

turned to the U.S. When his wife died, my brother married again. They had a child. He would divorce and remarry twice more but have no more children.

After leaving the military, my brother worked briefly with my father and then became a heavily bearded mystic. His life was erratic, at best. He lived off my grandmother's trust, convincing his wives (and perhaps himself) that there was a lot more money than there really was.

I was not prepared to cover my brother's lifestyle expenses but did pay for him to go to an addiction treatment center. His stay there was brief, with no lasting results. He died in 1993 at age 58. The funeral was interesting; his wife and exes kept asking me about that nonexistent fortune.

I did feel some responsibility for my brother's young children, including the two adopted ones. Why should they suffer for his poor choices?

During the 70s, the adopted children were struggling in their home setting. My parents couldn't help, so the kids moved in with me and my family for a while. When we later set up trusts for my nieces and nephew, we included them too even though they weren't blood relatives.

The point of that rather long story is that defining family and family responsibilities has lots of gray areas. We each have to do what we think is right. "Don't help those who won't help themselves" and "Do help those who can't help themselves" may sum it up for me.

FALLACY 3—TOP-DOWN FAMILY GOVERNANCE

I HAVE HAD many interesting discussions on this subject with Tom Rogerson, who now is a wealth strategist focused on family governance and education at Wilmington Trust. Sometimes we agree, and sometimes not. Sometimes we agree in principle, but I can't imagine applying it to my own family.

Tom makes a compelling case for the importance of family dynamics, referring to a survey of risks to family wealth conducted by the Williams Group, a family wealth consultancy in San Clemente, California. What causes that dreaded shirtsleeves to shirtsleeves wealth problem?

Here's what the survey said: 60% of the failure is due to a lack of communication and trust around decision making and governance, and 25% of the failure can be attributed to unprepared heirs. Only 3% of failure can be blamed on financial planning, taxes and investments.

Aha, the professionals would say, a failure of family leadership. You need a family council, a family mission statement, family values, family meetings, family philanthropy, career planning for family members, and a leadership succession plan. You need family governance!

I understand the problem; families are complicated. Even excluding the in-laws, there are multiple relationships, coalitions and competitions. Birth order, gender, innate skills and dozens of other factors affect the dynamics. Add the in-laws, and the complexities are mind-boggling.

However, I disagree with the proposed solution—family governance—for a number of reasons. First, there's that pesky problem of who is family, as discussed above.

Second, that model takes away individuals' rights and responsibilities to manage their own destinies, make their own mistakes, and even change their own minds.

What emerges is the tyranny of the majority or the iron-handed rule of a patriarch or matriarch. Both approaches can lead to narrow definitions of success for family members (e.g., thou shalt follow my example) and hierarchies among presumed equals. In-laws may be shunned (think out-laws).

Take trusts, for example. They can be a useful tool but in some cases, they would more aptly be called "mis-trusts."

I know someone who set up a family trust with strict distribution rules (e.g., second spouses were out). Another person set up a 1,000 year trust. That suggests he believes that William the Conqueror's wisdom would still apply for another 51 years (as of 2015) if he set up a trust in 1066.

Third, family governance also presumes that family members share the same values.

That's certainly not the case in our family; I joke that our views range from Mother Teresa to Attila the Hun. Trying to force family values can result in people going along until escape is possible (which I call hypocrisy) or you can end up hating each other.

With a strong enough leader and enough money at stake, family differences may be submerged. But at the big bang, when the leader is gone, all of the dynamics noted above will resurface, possibly with a vengeance.

Tom concedes that family wealth professionals can do damage; lawyers mandating governance from the grave are one example. But he gently reminded me that "they" (i.e., wealth professionals) are not all alike, which is a fair point. So here is Tom's rebuttal to my rebuttal.

Tom hails from a family who managed to dissipate its wealth over a few generations. He agrees that you can't solve the shirtsleeves problem but argues that you can slow it down through education and integrated family wealth solutions.

One problem, he notes, is that most families strive to raise unique, independent and strong children while just assuming that the family is a team. Maybe, but probably not. Tom quotes George Burns: "Happiness is having a large, loving, close-knit family in another city."

You need to take concrete action to build a home team advantage, Tom asserts, much as you would with a management team at work.[42] It's a five step process: (1) education, (2) communication, (3) shared experiences/values, (4) philanthropy, and (5) governance.

Tom saw me cringe at governance and pointed out that basically it's just about decision making, and will happen regardless. (Anarchy is a form of governance.) He caught my attention with the notion of an entrepreneurial family, which works as a coalition, tapping into each other's resources.

Family philanthropy sparked another discussion. Tom sees it as a starting point for group decision making. You get everyone together, and decide where to donate a pot of money. (A family foundation is the ultimate version of that exercise.)

I am strongly committed to philanthropy and try to encourage it in my children but—yes, once again—I can't imagine consensus based on shared values. Instead, Fredi and I give each of our children a sum of money from our charitable trust each year, and let them decide what to support. (It varies.)

Tom then pointed out that you don't need to share values, citing Malcolm Gladwell's *Tipping Point* observation that affinity is more about shared experiences.[43] The aim with families is to build mutual understanding and respect, not preach or convert.

That led us to another cringe point: family meetings. Tom sees them as opportunities for getting to know each other better, perhaps through a

---

42. See "The Home Team Advantage: Successfully Preparing Your Family for the Future" by Tom Rogerson, Wilmington Trust (*www.wilmingtontrust.com/.../PDF/2013_Home_Team_Advantage.pdf*).
43. *The Tipping Point: How Little Things Can Make a Big Difference*, Malcom Gladwell, Little Brown, 2000.

boat-building team competition, or a family communication styles exercise. Some other professionals advocate a more business style meeting.

Either or both of those approaches may work for some families. Our family doesn't seem to feel the need; we get together socially often enough, and have many one-on-one interactions. And, with our crew, it's hard to imagine perfect harmony emerging from a mandatory all-family event.

Easy to criticize, you may say, but what to do? In the next chapter, I'll offer some conclusions I've reached about family wealth from my own experiences.

MY PHILOSOPHY OF FAMILY WEALTH

THANKSGIVING DINNER AT our house last year included Fredi, me, seven children and 14 grandchildren.[44] I feel it safe to say that we are wealthy enough to have real choices, and complex enough to experience most problems.

As I've reflected on our experiences—as well as my broader family experiences and what I have observed in other families—I've come to see that four main principles guide how I think about families and wealth. They are summarized in the following box and explained further in this chapter.

> **HOWARD'S PHILOSOPHY OF FAMILY WEALTH**
>
> 1. When it's about power, it's all over.
> 2. We are stronger together.
> 3. Family leaders are servant leaders.
> 4. The tree branches must—and will—thin.

---

44. That would be the simplest version of family that I can muster; there are a myriad of other players, as you saw if you made it through Part I of this book.

PRINCIPLE 1—WHEN IT'S ABOUT POWER, IT'S ALL OVER

TRADITIONAL FAMILY WEALTH models fly in the face of my general theory of everything. (See **Figure 9-1**.) It's a simple theory, really. It says that power and wealth drive people's behaviors. Competition or cooperation? Those are the two options.

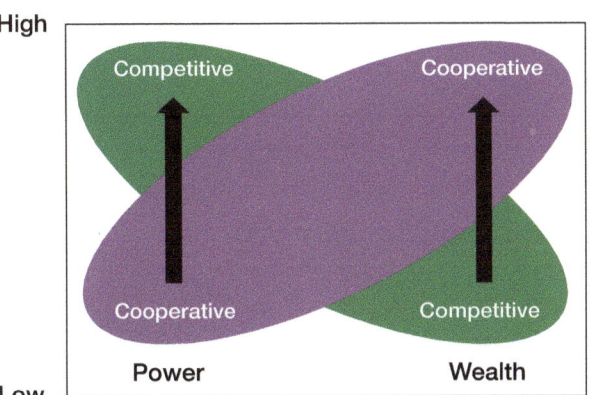

FIGURE 9-1
Howard's General Theory of Everything

I am not naïve. In Africa, power gets you wealth and in the United States, wealth gets you power. I submit, however, that the two dimensions—wealth and power—are very different.

People without resources will compete for what they can get. You can get day laborers for practically nothing, if they and their family are poor and hungry. Wealthy individuals can afford to be more cavalier. More importantly, they can cooperate to do deals.

Lack of power motivates people to band together. Mobs, unions and armies are responses to low individual power; they provide high collective power. At the high end of the power spectrum, individuals with power usually are not eager to share it much less give it up.

With wealthy families, the good news is that there's a lot to go around; that promotes unity and cooperation. If family members feel a certain degree of trust and individual freedom, you're probably in good shape. But start playing power games, and you're in trouble.

I believe that control by the older generation is a prime reason why families fall apart. What I call the "generation gap" is partly to blame. The older generation created the wealth, the thinking goes, so it should get to make the decisions and set the rules. Wealth is wielded like a weapon.

I am not a fan of using wealth to punish people for decisions that you don't like. Here's an example.

One Egyptian family sent the eldest son to Boston College, complete with Beacon Hill condo and Gucci charge card. When he announced that he didn't want to run the family business after graduating, they cut him off. (I do not believe that he returned to the fold.)

Members of the next generation will have their own goals, personalities, learning methods, talents, work habits, and attitudes towards money. They will live in a totally different world, one that will look different still for their children. They have a right to define their own success.

PRINCIPLE 2—WE ARE STRONGER TOGETHER

I BELIEVE THAT we are stronger together as a family. I like to illustrate that point with the story of the bundle of sticks. (See the box below.) I first heard it at a traditional Seder at a Jewish friend's house but it can be traced back to one of Aesop's Fables. The moral of the story is: "In unity is strength."

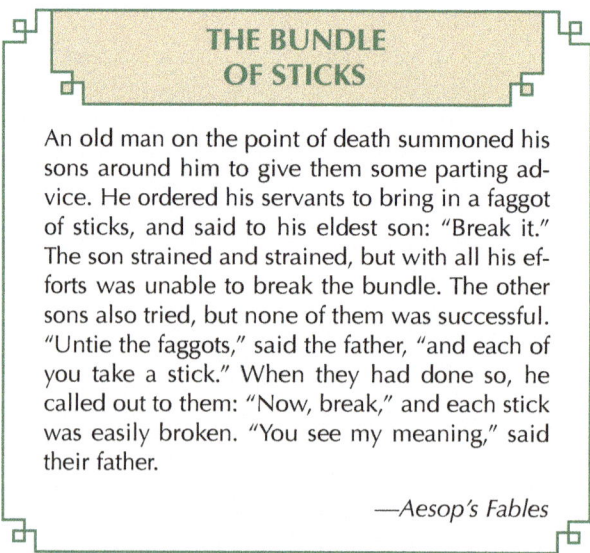

THE BUNDLE OF STICKS

An old man on the point of death summoned his sons around him to give them some parting advice. He ordered his servants to bring in a faggot of sticks, and said to his eldest son: "Break it." The son strained and strained, but with all his efforts was unable to break the bundle. The other sons also tried, but none of them was successful. "Untie the faggots," said the father, "and each of you take a stick." When they had done so, he called out to them: "Now, break," and each stick was easily broken. "You see my meaning," said their father.

—Aesop's Fables

I also believe that only voluntary associations work in the long run: "If you love me set me free. If I come back, it was meant to be." Variations of that popular theme have been attributed to Richard Bach (author of *Jonathan Livingston Seagull*) and appear in songs by Sting and Olivia Newton-John.

Our family's investing partnership, SFILP, is based on that premise. Participation is strongly encouraged but completely voluntary. So far, no one has declined the opportunity, recognizing the value of pooling time, talent and treasure for mutual benefit.

The nonfinancial benefits to strong family ties are equally if not more important, I believe.

In our family, we celebrate each other's successes. We rally for one another when the inevitable bad times come. We respect our differences, and tap into each of our unique strengths. We have fun together. In that sense, I fully agree with Tom Rogerson on the home team advantage.

PRINCIPLE 3—FAMILY LEADERS ARE SERVANT LEADERS

SERVANT LEADERSHIP IS a philosophy that goes back to the early Chinese dynasties, and was popularized in modern times by Robin Greenleaf.[45] It is the antithesis of hierarchical leadership and—in the context of families— the all-powerful patriarch or matriarch.

I believe that servant leadership captures our approach to our family's investment partnership.

Because participation is voluntary, the leader must earn family members' trust. (A leader, it has been said, is someone that others follow.) That requires the right mix of investing and interpersonal skills plus altruism; he or she is working on everyone's behalf.

Communication and education are critical tasks for servant leaders.

Family members must understand SFILP's value as a device for building and leveraging scale among our investment activities. (No one wants ten $50,000 accounts but they might take $500,000.) They also must be confident that the fund is well managed with no crazies involved.

---

45. Robert Greenleaf first coined the phrase in a 1970 essay called "The Servant as Leader."

Finally, they must have a realistic view of the partnership as a long term investment opportunity. They are free to withdraw funds but will lose the benefit of compounded growth. (The GPs can refuse a withdrawal if they judge it to be dangerous to portfolio liquidity, but we have not had to do so yet.)

Working with family can pose challenges, however. We don't have a formal set of rules so decisions tend to be on a case by case basis and get into value judgments.

For example, I established a trust at my mother's request for my brother's children within SFILP. When the youngest came of age and it was time to break up the trust, I wanted to let them stay in the partnership but my fellow GPs did not. (I did eventually win that one!)

We do not have formal all-partner meetings, instead issuing an annual letter explaining performance, strategic direction and industry trends. There also are frequent ad hoc consultations with individual family members at their request.

Andy likes to quip, "If you want your family to stay wealthy, have one kid. If you want to manage your wealth well, have seven kids." We hope that someone in the next (still young) generation will be willing and able to step up to fill his shoes, when the time comes.

PRINCIPLE 4—THE TREE BRANCHES MUST—AND WILL—THIN

AS I'VE SAID many times (and hopefully demonstrated), the wealth that you accumulate can't support an entire family forever. Does that imply ruthlessly cutting off some branches? As often is the case, the answer is, "Yes and no."

Wealth, as we said in *Chapter 5*, is a responsibility. How much, to whom, how and when are all difficult decisions sometimes. As a wealth owner, you make choices about how to allocate your finite resources. That may leave some family members unhappy.

It is even more likely that some branches will separate, no matter what you do.

Some branches of my family made valiant efforts to keep the clan together, including gatherings in Ogden, Utah on Memorial Day to decorate family graves. We had lots of family picnics growing up. I knew second and third cousins well.

Fifty-five years have passed. I have lived on the east coast for over fifty years. When I last was in Salt Lake, I did gather four out of five cousins for a lunch. We had little in common. I recently tried to reconnect with a third cousin living in New York City but got no response.

The lesson there: Thinning will happen all on its own, if relationships are voluntary. People may decide to align with another family or a different community altogether. You just have to be willing to let go.

Now, about the kids.

RAISING WEALTHY KIDS

THAYER WILLIS, A member of the family that founded Georgia–Pacific Corporation, claims that family wealth can be a blessing and a curse.[46] I tend to agree with that, although I must point out that it's not the money that deserves the blame or credit; it's what you do with it.

Family wealth is a tricky thing, especially when there are significant differences between the older and younger generations' circumstances and perspectives. Here are some interesting factoids from a wealth survey:[47]

- The majority of wealthy people (78%) achieved financial success by creating it, not inheriting it; and at least half (52%) grew up in middle class or lower middle class households.

- Their heirs are more likely to grow up wealthy. More than half of surveyed millennials (ages 18–33) were second or third generation wealthy, and 48% already had an inheritance.

- Almost all parents (96%) thought their children weren't mature enough to handle family money until at least age 25, and only 38%

---

46. Thayer Willis is the author of *Navigating the Dark Side of Wealth: A Life Guide for Inheritors* (New Concord Press, 2003) and *Beyond Gold: True Wealth for Inheritors* (New Concord Press, 2012).
47. 2012 Harris Poll Youth Plus. "$211 Billion and So Much to Buy—American Youths, the New Big Spenders" (October 26, 2011).

of parents with children over that age had fully disclosed their financial status.

◆ Only 38% of parents of children of all ages strongly agreed that their children would be well prepared to handle the inheritance planned for them.

With that as a sobering backdrop, this chapter will consider some of the challenges faced by wealthy parents, and share my response to a daughter-in-law who requested my advice for future generations.

CHALLENGES FOR WEALTHY PARENTS

HOW TO RAISE healthy, functioning kids in the context of wealth is a question that keeps a lot of rich parents up at night. Six common challenges are listed in the accompanying box and briefly discussed below. As always, I claim no Solomonic wisdom but am happy to share my experience.

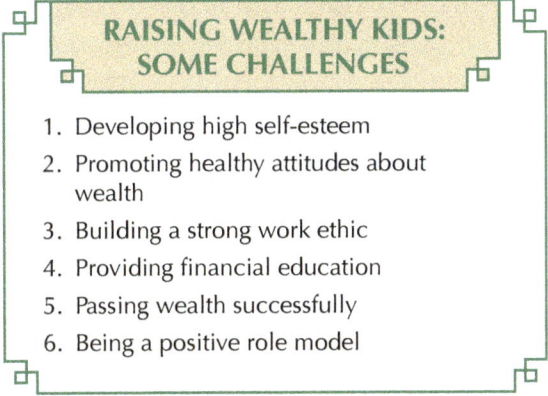

RAISING WEALTHY KIDS: SOME CHALLENGES

1. Developing high self-esteem
2. Promoting healthy attitudes about wealth
3. Building a strong work ethic
4. Providing financial education
5. Passing wealth successfully
6. Being a positive role model

Challenge 1—Developing High Self-Esteem

Self-esteem is a judgment about your own worth as a person. The challenge for wealthy families is how not to let the family name, reputation and money define its members. Every child—rich, poor or in between—needs to develop his or her own identity and feelings of self-worth.

Tom Rogerson points out that one of the worst things a parent can do is to "withhold the gifts of responsibility and accountability." Abraham

Lincoln put it this way: "The worst thing you can do for those you love is the things they could do for themselves."

The hard part can be trusting your children's judgment enough to allow moderate failures. Coaching them to be thoughtful, confident decision-makers can help.

One of my sons recalls that my response whenever he came to me with some sort of decision or plan was, "Did you think it through?" (He also jokes that if I said it twice, it was not a good sign.) If I liked it, I would say, "If you have thought it through, go ahead."

Another way to build self-esteem is to foster individuality, while building a culture of mutual respect and interdependence among family members. (Yes, that home team again.)

Making sure that everyone has a place in the sun where they can succeed, and celebrating those successes is important. As part of that process, you need to help each child develop self-awareness—an understanding of what is important to her, as well as her unique strengths and weaknesses.

It is important to appreciate and use the differences among your children too. Many families compete first among themselves, and only then with the outside world. Fostering intense competition within the family may make the individuals stronger but won't strengthen the team.

Challenge 2—Promoting Healthy Attitudes about Wealth

Unhealthy attitudes about wealth are easy but painful to see. They range from shame and guilt ("Children are starving in India.") to entitlement and apathy ("Yes, I could walk but I'll take the Porsche.") or arrogance and ingratitude ("Why can't I have EXACTLY what I want, NOW?!").

At their worst, they lead to "affluenza" as a legal defense in a Texas teenager's drunk driving manslaughter case. (The argument was that the teenager was unable to link his bad behavior with consequences because his parents had taught him that wealth buys privilege.)

By healthy attitudes, I mean appreciating that wealth is a gift, not a right, and most definitely not a certainty; that wealth is a means to an ends, not a measure of success; and that wealth does not make you better than other people.

I have found that living in an economically diverse place can help. The diversity can help prevent wealth myopia ("Isn't everyone rich?"), and provide different models of success.

That was a valuable experience for me as I was growing up, and I tried to provide the same experience for my young family. I wanted my boys to be raised in a comfortable but not extravagant lifestyle. The parents of their friends included firemen and salesmen.

Other common problems include using money and things as an expression of love. (Remember that Beatles' song, "Can't Buy Me Love?") Then there's the focus on always having "the best" (i.e., the most expensive), which can lead to materialism and spending beyond your means.

Making money a taboo subject does not contribute to healthy attitudes about wealth either.

Family money matters may be private, but private is different from secret. One parent proudly told me that he forged his kids' signatures on their tax returns so they wouldn't see their income. The fact that their grandmother's name was on the town museum supposedly was lost on them.

Young people often overestimate the family's wealth when it's not discussed. Talking about money in an open, matter of fact way gives them a realistic view of what you do and don't have. They don't have to resort to Google searches or friends' guesses.

Challenge 3—Building a Strong Work Ethic

Thayer, who says that she "frittered away her 20s, living as a hippie," offers a good description of the problem:

> *The biggest curse of intergenerational wealth ... is the illusion that you don't have to do much with your life. You might want to and you might make the effort, but you don't have the same pressure to earn enough to live on. And that takes away a lot of the incentive to find meaningful work ....*

I recognized that problem early on, when my sons were still young. I wanted to avoid the "trustafarian" syndrome that I first witnessed at Stanford. I've listened to parents bewail the fact that their kid is a ski bum in Aspen. The child's puzzled response, "You said you wanted me to be happy. I'm happy."

By the time they were twelve, my sons were earning money from lawn mowing and other chores. During summer vacations, they enjoyed family vacations (a trip to France to visit my AFS family was a special treat) but also had various jobs.

I gave a lot of thought to the question of inheritance for my children. The goal is for it to be enough to provide them with choices but not enough to allow them to be lazy. They actually like to work, which is something I'm proud of.

Challenge 4—Providing Financial Education

Financial education for children and youth is a hot topic these days, for good reason.

Our nation's young people spend an estimated $211 billion annually[48] and have rising debt along with a poor inclination to save. It's the time when they are (or are not) developing the knowledge, skills and behaviors needed to be financially responsible adults.

Who is responsible for educating your kids?

Some people feel that there should be more (or at least some) personal finance education in high schools, universities, even business schools. There are, in fact, many initiatives underway to develop policies and programs including curriculum development and competency testing.

Still, I and many others agree that the primary responsibility falls to the parents.

One parent took it upon himself to write a book about personal money management to pass on to his five kids. *Why Didn't They Teach Me This in School? 99 Personal Money Management Principles to Live By*[49] is a hot gift for high school and college grads (according to Amazon).

I sometimes recommend Joline Godfrey's *Raising Financially Fit Kids*. It covers ten core skills across five developmental stages (childhood,

---

48. 2012 Harris Poll Youth Plus. "$211 Billion and So Much to Buy – American Youths, the New Big Spenders" (October 26, 2011).
49. *Why Didn't They Teach Me This in School? 99 Personal Money Management Principles to Live By*, Cary Siegel, Create Space, 2013.

tweens, middle school, high school, 20-somethings). Its big ideas include living within one's means, and our responsibility as global citizens to give back.

Still—unfortunately—money is right up there with sex when it comes to unpopular subjects at the dinner table, especially for wealthy families. But it can start with simple concepts and teachable moments. Here are a few examples, from my experience.

"One dollar can't serve two purposes." A friend taught that lesson to his young children by giving them a weekly allowance, and having them divide it up among three jars—one for spending, one for saving, and one for charity. Not a bad discipline to instill, in my opinion.

When my first son turned sixteen, I decided to run what some friends considered a bold and even foolhardy experiment. I handed him a check and said, "Go buy a car for the family, some sort of Audi." I figured it would be a good educational experience and say "I trust you."

He was amazing. (He was motivated because he knew he would get the used car.) He checked Blue Book values, went to ten dealers, researched the packages needed, reviewed dealer service records, negotiated deals, and came back with recommendations. We discussed them, and I signed up for one. (I haven't negotiated for a car since.)

When I invited my two local sons who were interested to join me as GPs of SFILP, it was partly to help me with the administrative burden but also to educate them for their financial responsibilities; a way to pass on my expertise and values. They were 29 and 33 at the time, and have done a great job.

Basically, I've tried to help my kids understand the mechanics of wealth, and how to think about what they need to finance their lifestyles. They talk about living below their means, which I believe is a good thing, and now are thinking about a model for the next generation.

I should mention that I consider philanthropy an important subject for financial education. Fredi and I are very active, and encourage our children to contribute their time, talent and networks as well as financial resources to causes they care about.

Formal education about philanthropy also is emerging.

My 9th grade grandson participates in a Youth in Philanthropy course at school. The Buffett family's Learning by Giving Foundation focuses on college students. Its Giving with Purpose course includes a $10,000 fund to invest in local organizations through a peer review competition.

Challenge 5—Passing Wealth Successfully

The question that seems to provoke the most anxiety among wealthy parents is: When and how to tell them?

I strongly believe that it's better to start the discussions before your children start making important life decisions. Respect for money can and should be engrained at an early age. It's the difference between talking about a $20 toy at age ten and a really expensive purchase at age 20.

It should be a process, not a grand event. You are preparing them for life, not to be inheritors. Context is key. Parents often put the cart before the horse. "I'm worth $100 million" is not helpful but a thoughtful discussion on "what is wealth?" can start building an important foundation.

Another big question is: How much to give them?

I am in the same philosophical camp as Warren Buffett, whose response was, "Enough to do anything they want but not enough to do nothing." My oft-repeated message to my children is, "I have given you money so you can have a choice, but only you can develop a feeling of accomplishment."

That still begs the math question: How much is enough?

Bill Gates is rumored to have defined that as $10 million, which is still a drop in his wealth bucket. For my children, I settled on a smaller number, of course, but enough that the annual yield on it plus the earnings from virtually any career would make them not rich, but solidly middle class.

Then there's the question of when to pass wealth on to the next generation. I believe in making money available when it can be useful. With my sons, I decided to distribute trusts at ages 30 and 35, figuring they would have a sense of what they wanted to do with their lives by then.

At the end of the day, each of us who is fortunate enough to have wealth to pass on must decide what we feel is right and hope for the best, recognizing that the recipients may or may not agree. The best you can do is to be clear about your intentions . . . and tell them that you love them.

Challenge 6—Being a Positive Role Model

"Walk the talk" is a well-worn but invaluable piece of advice. There also is great wisdom in one of my grandmother's favorite sayings, "Your actions speak so loudly that I cannot hear a word you say." Still another useful, if unattributed, observation is: "Values are caught, not taught."

Role modeling is an important but difficult tool. It requires behaving in a way that is consistent with the philosophy that you espouse, in your day-to-day actions and interactions with others. Kids do notice . . . and imitate. (A lot of wealthy parents know that they are setting a bad example.)

As a parent, your time may be your scarcest resource but time is critical for teaching by example. You have to schedule time for family-time activities and give your full attention. (I agree with Tom on that.) And you have to try to balance approval and acceptance, with teaching and constructive criticism.

I try not to preach, but rather to be open to and available for questions as they arise, and help my children come to their own conclusions. Unsolicited advice is rarely appreciated or useful, I find. The recipient likely will get resentful and rebel, with the advice giver left feeling rejected.

A final important point: Your kids are not you. Role modeling is not about engineering "mini-me's." Children will—and should—have many role models in their lives. In *Howard's Gift*, we call that "the mosaic in the mirror."

It's always interesting to have your children tell you what they have learned from you. It's not always what you might expect or hope for. But as in the example in the box on the next page, offered to me by one of my sons as a Christmas gift, it can be very heartwarming.

ADVICE FOR FUTURE GENERATIONS

AS I WAS writing *Howard's Journey*, one family member posed this question: "I wonder, Howard, what questions would you want your grandchildren to ask themselves, at various points in their lives?" Well, that's an interesting question!

My answer started with this quote:

If I am not for myself, who will be for me? But if I am only for myself, who am I? If not now, when?

Spoken many centuries ago by Hillel, a Jewish religious leader, these words counsel each of us to find our unique self and share it with the world . . . and not dillydally about it. I think the questions are quite profound and useful, at whatever age you may be.

I wish each member of my family success. And therein lies the challenge and another question: What is success, and how do you attain it?

> **TEACHINGS AND LEARNINGS, FROM THE NEXT GENERATION**
>
> You're a great teacher of life. So you have far taught us that
>
> *Time spent with family is as valuable as time spent alone.*
>
> *New isn't always the answer.*
>
> *Education is for a lifetime.*
>
> *Knowing how to do it yourself is critical, but sometimes you should hire others.*
>
> *Patience and persistence are needed in all jobs.*
>
> *Teaching our children how to use tools gives them a lifetime of opportunities.*
>
> *To plan and what a plan represents.*
>
> *Indulgence is not always bad.*
>
> *Sharing with others is rewarding.*
>
> *Building and sharing values creates a community.*
>
> *Economic gain is not the only measure.*
>
> *Having all the toys isn't the point – having fun is.*
>
> *Working hard can be a reward unto itself.*
>
> *Teaching someone to learn is one of the best gifts.*

I haven't found a better framework for tackling that question than *Just Enough*, the book that Laura Nash and I wrote some years ago. We were interested in real, enduring success—where getting what you want yields rewards that are sustainable for you and the people you care about.

Our research showed there is no one right answer. It also showed that enduring success has four dimensions: significance, legacy, achievement and happiness. As shown in **Figure 10-1** on the next page, each dimension presents a challenging question for each of us to answer, as we work to define our unique vision of success.

Now, here's where the quest for success gets really interesting.

It turns out that the single-minded pursuit of any one component won't work; to achieve enduring success each person must hit each one with some regularity. Also, you need "just enough" of each to attain enduring success, and you must set the standard for enough.

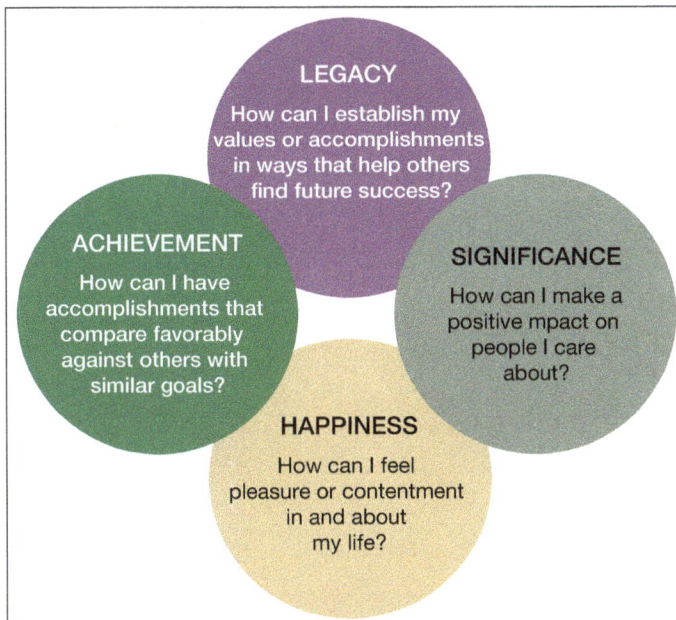

FIGURE 10-1
Enduring Success: Dimensions and Questions

Source: *Just Enough: Tools for Creating Success in Your Work and Life*

Success That Lasts, an article based on *Just Enough*, offers an exercise designed to help you create your own kaleidoscope. (If you're interested, it was in the February 2004 issue of *Harvard Business Review*.)

You can use it to analyze your success patterns, and for planning. What would a satisfying life look like? What goals or activities can help you achieve just enough in all four circles? Presented with an opportunity or a choice, where would it fit in your vision of success?

It's important to revisit your vision and strategies for success as you and your circumstances change. You're not likely to want the same things at 80 or 60 as at 40 or 20, unless you are Hugh Hefner.[49]

And, opportunities will arise when and where you least expect them.

Setting goals and taking action require luck, skill and some degree of courage. You may not always win, but you will have the satisfaction of knowing you tried.

---

49. Hefner is the founder of the *Playboy* empire.

My mother often quoted John Greenleaf Whittier: "For of all sad words of tongue or pen, the saddest are these: It might have been!" I don't regret anything I've done in my life but I've always feared that I would regret it if I *didn't* try something.

If any or all of that sounds daunting, allow me to offer some practical advice from Arthur Ashe, the great tennis player struck down by a deadly disease. Before he died, he was asked how he dealt with his illness. His answer, "Start from where you are. Use what you have. Do what you can do."

Now, on to this book's Conclusion.

CONCLUSION: THE GAME OF LIFE

IT SEEMS FITTING to come full circle to the subject of life journeys as the conclusion to this book. It is after all based on the family book, *Howard's Journey: My Game of Life*. The game metaphor inspired us to use a Monopoly board to represent my life's journey on the book cover.

I had a lot of fun creating "Howardopoly." It is shown on the next page as **Figure C-1**. (It looks much nicer in a larger size.)

As I told my family members, we each create our own version. The layout of each person's board, the skill and luck cards, and the throws of the dice will be different from mine. The rules of the game, however, are the same for all: Throw the dice, see where you land, draw cards, and keep playing.

We included some "tips for winning" on the dust jacket for the family book. They bear listing here, in the box below, along with the reminder that it's the journey that really matters, not the destination.

TIPS FOR WINNING AT THE GAME OF LIFE

1. Make your own scorecard.
2. Play fair.
3. Accept what happens.
4. Learn from the past to change the future.
5. Be appreciative, and show it.
6. Tell the people you love, "I love you."
7. Don't accept the status quo.
8. Beware of experts.
9. Leave the world a little better for passing through.
10. Have fun!

FIGURE C-1
Howardopoly: My Game of Life

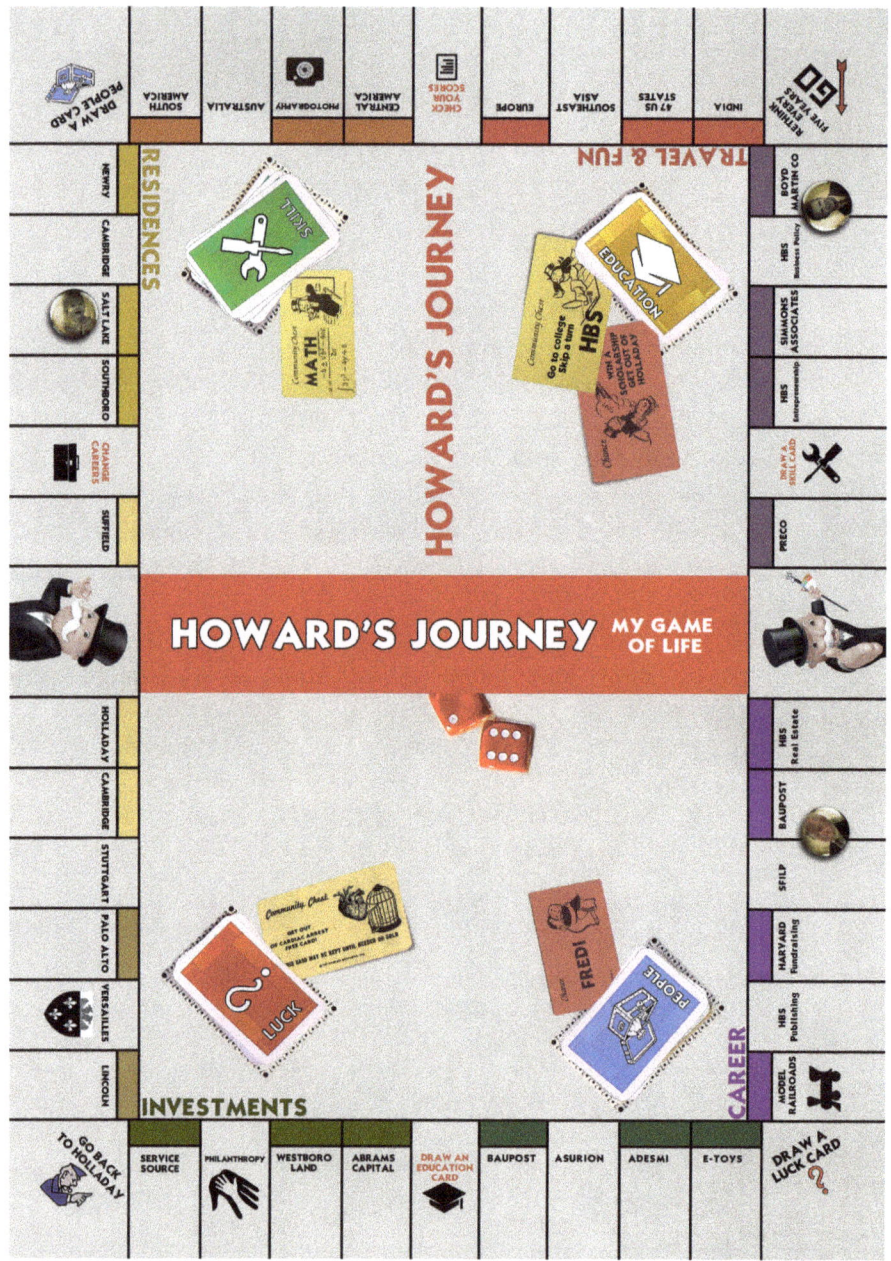

On a somewhat more serious note, I also shared with my family an ancient Sanskrit poem that I love and used to close the last MBA class that I taught at HBS. (See the box below.) It is called "Salutation to the Dawn."

The poem reminds us that all we really have is today, "for yesterday is but a dream, and tomorrow only a vision."

More wise counsel follows: "Look to this day!" Even the dark ones may have some brighter moments, and any day—good or bad—can be a learning experience.

I hope that you enjoy "Salutation to the Dawn" and take it to heart as your life's journey unfolds, one day at a time.

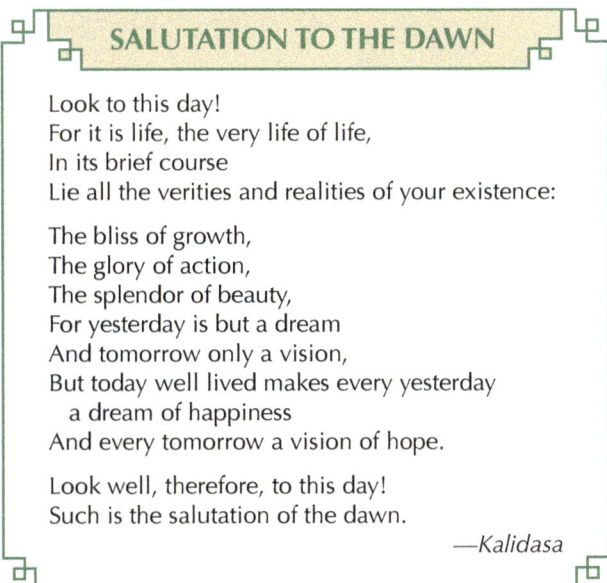

SALUTATION TO THE DAWN

Look to this day!
For it is life, the very life of life,
In its brief course
Lie all the verities and realities of your existence:

The bliss of growth,
The glory of action,
The splendor of beauty,
For yesterday is but a dream
And tomorrow only a vision,
But today well lived makes every yesterday
   a dream of happiness
And every tomorrow a vision of hope.

Look well, therefore, to this day!
Such is the salutation of the dawn.

—Kalidasa

APPENDIX: WEALTH QUOTATIONS

WEALTH QUOTES

The greatest wealth is to live content with little.
—Plato

If a man is proud of his wealth, he should not be praised until it is known how he employs it.
—Socrates

Be careful to leave your sons well instructed rather than rich, for the hopes of the instructed are better than the wealth of the ignorant.
—Epictetus

Where there are friends there is wealth.
—Plautus

The only wealth which you will keep forever is the wealth you have given away.
—Marcus Aurelius

For many men, the acquisition of wealth does not end their troubles, it only changes them.
—Lucius Annaeus Seneca

Health is the greatest gift, contentment the greatest wealth, faithfulness the best relationship.
—Buddha

It is health that is real wealth and not pieces of gold and silver.
—Mahatma Gandhi

The possession of material riches, without inner peace, is like dying of thirst while bathing in a lake.
—Yogananda

A person's true wealth is the good he or she does in the world.
—Mohammed

Wealth is any income that is at least one hundred dollars more a year than the income of one's wife's sister's husband.
—H. L. Mencken

If we command our wealth, we shall be rich and free; if our wealth commands us, we are poor indeed.
—Edmund Burke

We make a living by what we get, but we make a life by what we give.
—Winston Churchill

Get to know two things about a man. How he earns his money and how he spends it. You will then have the clue to his character. You will have a searchlight that shows up the inmost recesses of his soul. You will know all you need to know about his standards, his motives, his driving desires, his real religion.
—Robert J. McCracken

(Cont'd)

WEALTH QUOTES (Cont'd)

If you want to know what a man is really like, take notice of how he acts when he loses money.
—Simone Weil

Wealth is the ability to fully experience life.
—Henry David Thoreau

The price of anything is the amount of life you exchange for it.
—Henry David Thoreau

Wealth is not his that has it, but his that enjoys it.
—Benjamin Franklin

Wealth is not without its advantages and the case to the contrary, although it has often been made, has never proved widely persuasive.
—John Kenneth Galbraith

I remember thinking quite logically that I didn't want to spoil my children with wealth and so that I would create a foundation.
—Bill Gates

The person who doesn't know where his next dollar is coming from usually doesn't know where his last dollar went.
—Unknown

With money you can buy a house, but not a home.
—Chinese Proverb

iver poisoned, you will find you cannot eat your money.
—Canadian Proverb

Some people are masters of money, and some people are slaves of it.
—Russian Proverb

One cannot both feast and become rich.
– African proverb

ACKNOWLEDGMENTS

GIVING CREDIT WHERE credit is due is hard for any author but is especially challenging for this book because it covers multiple subjects and a lifetime of experiences, and the influencers were both positive and negative.

Wealth and Families is a compilation based on 65 years of thinking about, worrying about and managing money; and 46 years of thinking about children, grandchildren, my community responsibilities, and the legacy I would hope to leave.

This book likely wouldn't have reached completion or garnered praise from at least one reader for its "pithy, pointed writing style" without the great work of my co-author, Shirley Spence. It would not look as nice without the design talents of Bonnie Van Slyke and Jereann Zann.

But it all started with my daughter-in-law, asking me to share what I have learned about investing and life for the benefit of the grandchildren. Then it required the patience of my wife and family, who didn't begrudge me the time it took to ponder what I have learned.

I have learned so many positive things from so many people. I have tried to acknowledge many of you in this book but inevitably will have left out some who contributed to the thinking that is reflected in *Wealth and Families*.

Some, like Bill Poorvu, Mike Roberts, Seth Klarman, Rob Freeman, Stuart Lucas, Tom Rogerson, Eileen Shapiro, Philippe and Nan-b de Gaspé Beaubien, and Roger and Colleen Allard have been constants in my life for over 30 years. We have exchanged many ideas and not always agreed on some of them.

Then there are people like Irv Grousbeck, Michael O'Connell, Roy Little, Craig Burr and Bill Egan. Our episodic interactions have profoundly changed my thinking. They are superstars in the investment world who have transmitted their values and knowledge to the next generation.

Now, the other side of the coin. I have a Wall Street Journal cartoon in my office that shows two people facing each other. One says to the other, "I learn from the mistakes of others. And you've been a real blessing."

Many people have given me insights as to what *not* to do when it comes to wealth and families. Their actions often came out of love but the outcomes sometimes were sad. I hope that what I recount in this book—including my mistakes—may help others to avoid unnecessary pitfalls.

Finally, I must acknowledge my children and grandchildren. I am hoping that what I have shared will be helpful I to them. I want them to know that I have learned much from them, and thank them for that. As one grandson said, "We're a really lucky family, to be together."

Most of all, thank you, Fredi!

AUTHOR BIOGRAPHIES

Howard Stevenson

HOWARD HAS MADE and managed his own money for himself and his family. He also is deeply committed to philanthropy as a donor, board member and fundraiser. Harvard Business School (HBS) has been the nexus of a career that has included entrepreneurial ventures in real estate and investing.

Howard was the founder and first president of the Baupost Group, Inc., which manages partnerships investing in liquid securities for wealthy families. He now serves as Advisory Board co-chair of Baupost LLC, a $29 billion registered investment company.

As a professor at Harvard Business School, Howard touched the lives of thousands of students and held several leadership positions. He is considered the founding father of entrepreneurial management at HBS. Upon his recent retirement, a chair was named in his honor.

Howard also is the author of thirteen books and hundreds of articles and case studies. (See the box on the next page.) His most cherished role, however, is as the member of a family that he describes as "wealthy enough to have real choices and complex enough to face real challenges."

Shirley Spence

SHIRLEY BEGAN WORKING with Howard as a research associate at HBS. She has collaborated with him on several projects including the family book upon which *Wealth and Families* is based, and *Getting to Giving: Fundraising the Entrepreneurial Way.*

A graduate of Dartmouth College and the Harvard Graduate School of Education, her career has included teaching high school French, brand management at Procter & Gamble, case writing at HBS, and a partner position at Mercer Management Consulting (now Oliver Wyman).

Shirley's work and personal interests have afforded her the pleasure of visiting many parts of the globe, and meeting a wide variety of people. Her passions are a love of learning, and the joy of enabling others to learn and share their learnings.

HOWARD'S BOOKSHELF

Wealth and Families: Lessons from My Life Journey, Howard H. Stevenson with Shirley Spence, Timberline Management, Belmont, MA: 2016.

Getting to Giving: Fundraising the Entrepreneurial Way, Howard H. Stevenson with Shirley Spence, Timberline Management, Belmont, MA: 2011.

Entrepreneurship in the Social Sector, Jane Wei-Skillern, James E. Austin, Herman Leonard, and Howard Stevenson, Sage Publications, Thousand Oaks, CA: 2007.

Make Your Own Luck: 12 Practial Steps to Taking Smarter Risks in Business, Eileen C. Shapiro and Howard H. Stevenson, Penguin Group, New York: 2005.

Just Enough: Tools for Creating Success in Your Work and Life, Laura Nash and Howard Stevenson. John Wiley & Sons, Inc., New York: 2004.

Winning Angels: The Seven Fundamentals of Early-stage Investing, David Amis and Howard H. Stevenson, Pearson Education: Financial Times/Prentice Hall, London: 2001.

Do Lunch or Be Lunch: The Power of Predictability in Creating Your Future, Howard H. Stevenson with Jeffrey L. Cruikshank, Harvard Business School Press, Boston: 1997.

The Entrepreneurial Venture, 2nd Edition, Readings selected by William A. Sahlman, Howard H. Stevenson, Michael J. Roberts, and Amar Bhidé, Harvard Business School Publishing, Boston: 1999.

The Entrepreneurial Venture, Readings selected by William A. Sahlman and Howard H. Stevenson, Harvard Business School Publishing, Boston: 1994.

New Business Ventures and the Entrepreneur, Howard H. Stevenson, Michael J. Roberts, Irving Grousbeck, and A. Bhidé, R. D. Irwin, Inc., Homewood, IL: 1985, 1989, 1994, 1999.

New Business Ventures and the Entrepreneur (Instructor's Manual), Howard H. Stevenson, Michael J. Roberts, H. Irving Grousbeck, and A. Bhidé, R. D. Irwin, Inc., Homewood, IL: 1985, 1989, 1994, 1999.

Policy Formulation and Administration, Howard H. Stevenson, C. R. Christensen, N. Berg, and M. Salter, R. D. Irwin, Inc., Homewood, IL: 1984.

Policy Formulation and Administration (Instructor's Manual), Howard H. Stevenson, C. R. Christensen, N. Berg, and M. Salter, R. D. Irwin, Inc., Homewood, IL: 1984.

INDEX

Numbers followed by *i* in italics refer to pages with images.

A

accountability
  children's learning of, 109–10
  financial future and, 50, 57, 85–86
  Mormon approach to, 12, 24
  as one of Howard's six truths, 33, 34–35
accountants, 76, 77, 78*t*
achievement, as success dimension, 116, 117*f*
actions, as good bets (one of Howard's six truths), 33, 38–39
Adams, Scott, 46, 70, 71, 87
adopted children, 97, 98
advisors, 76, 77, 78, 79n, 81, 82, 85
Aesop's Fables, 104
affluenza, 110
African proverb, 123
age of accountability, in Mormon Church, 12, 34
Alice's Adventures in Wonderland (Carroll), 58
American Field Service (AFS) program, 12, 112
American Research and Development (ARD), 42
anchor investments, 73
Arbor Health Care, 68
art, as investment, 43, 44
asset-based fees, 78*t*, 82, 83
assets
  goals and structuring, 59–60
  net worth and, 60
  wealth management scorecards and, 65
attitudes toward wealth, 109, 110–11
Auerbach, Isaac, 23
Aurelius, Marcus, 122

B

Bach, Richard, 105

banks
  investment banking, 16, 20
  wealth management and, 60, 77
Barton, George, 13
Baruch, Jordan, 23
Baupost Group, 23–25, 24*i*, 29, 36, 49, 53, 64, 65, 68, 69–70, 73, 84
Beatles, 111
Bessemer Securities, 43, 70, 74
bets and betting
  actions as good (one of Howard's six truths), 33, 38–39
  errors in, 38
  investment decision's similarities to, 38, 70, 72, 73, 74, 84
Beyer, Charlotte B., 79n
Biller, Bruce, 28
Booth School of Business, University of Chicago, 79
Borra, Pier, 68
Boston Consulting Group, 77
Boston Safe Deposit and Trust, 19
bottom line, 47*f*, 55
Boyd Martin Company, 11
British Isles, Stevenson family roots in, 5
brokerages, 77, 82
brokers, 77, 78*t*, 79n
Buddha, 122
Buffett, Warren, 114
Buffett family, 113
Building a Business in the Context of a Life (BBCL), Harvard Business School, 28, 59, 61, 63
Burke, Edmund, 122
Burns, George, 100
business income, 48–49

C

Canadian proverb, 123
carrying costs, 44
case method, at HBS, 15–16, 19, 22

case study
  of SFILP investing, 73–75
  of wealth management, 63–66
cash flow, 42, 49, 60, 65, 82
change, 22–23
  one of Howard's six truths, 8, 22, 33, 35–36, 63
  personal, over a lifetime, 8, 117
  planning and, 63
Chaos: Making a New Science (Gleick), 22–23
charitable giving, 60, 61, 66, 113. *See also* philanthropy
charitable trusts, 26, 53, 54, 66, 100
children. *See also* wealthy kids
  financial education for working with, 80
  financial responsibility to, 57
  raising in context of wealth, 2, 108–18
Chinese proverb, 123
choice, wealth as instrument of, 57–58
Churchill, Winston, 62, 122
community, 61
  concentric circles of, 57
  financial responsibility to, 57, 59, 63
  land conservation commitment and, 25
  Mormon values on, 12
  philanthropic gifts to, 64, 54
compounding, 42, 43, 53, 60, 91–92, 106
Connecticut General, 20
Cruikshank, Jeffrey L., 21n, 23n
Curtis, Jack, 13
cynicism, 36, 88

D

Dee family, 8, 91
"Defining Corporate Strengths and Weaknesses" (Stevenson), 16
definitions of wealth
  Howard's, 42–46
  traditional, 41–42
Digital Equipment Corporation (DEC), 42

Dilbert comic strip, 46, 71, 87
diminishing assets, 42, 43
distributions, 49, 53, 60, 99
diversification, 46, 70, 72, 73
divorce, and trusts, 25, 60, 92
Do Lunch or Be Lunch: The Power of Predictability in Creating Your Future (Stevenson and Cruikshank), 23n
Doomsday Book, 5
Duffy, Paula, 22

E

earned income, 48
educational opportunities, in wealth management, 79–80, 82
Einstein, Albert, 42
Eisenhower, Dwight D., 62
Eisenmann, Tom, 29
Ellenberg, Daniel, 70
emotions. *See* feelings
England, Stevenson family roots in, 5
"Entrepreneurial Management's Need for a More 'Chaotic' Theory" (Stevenson and Harmeling), 23
entrepreneurship, 50
  Howard's interest in, 20n, 22, 23, 29
  investing's similarities to, 71–72
entrepreneurship course, at HBS, 21–22, 21n, 26, 32, 68
Epictetus, 122
estate planning, 60, 64, 82
estate taxes, 55, 64
ethical factor, in selecting service providers, 84
experience factor, in selecting service providers, 85

F

family
  adopted children in, 97, 98
  bundle of sticks proverb about strength in, 104
  complexity of relationships in, 88, 98, 99
  defining responsibilities in, 97, 98

family (cont'd)
  differences between the older and younger generations' circumstances and perspectives in, 108–09
  financial responsibility to, 57, 64
  informal gatherings of, 106–07
  issues in defining members of, 89, 95–98, 99
  kids in. *See* wealthy kids
  meetings of, 100–01
  stepchildren in blended, 25, 97
  strength of members in, 102, 104–105
  traditional emphasis on bloodlines in, 95, 98
  vacations with, 112
  wealth goals and, 63, 64
family trees, 95–97
  dilemmas in using, 97
  new approach to representing, 96–97, 96t
  traditional approach to, 95–96, 95t
family wealth, 88–118
  bundle of sticks proverb about strength in, 104
  children and, 108–18
  Howard's philosophy of, 102–07
  leadership in, 105–106
  power issues and, 103–04
  rebuttal to models of, 89–101
  separation and thinning of branches in, 106–07
  strength of members in, 104–105
  voluntary associations in, 105
family wealth counselors, 78t
family wealth models, 89–101
  definition of, 95–98
  multigenerational, 89–95, 92t
  top-down governance in, 98–101
feelings
  of accomplishment, 114
  about money, 40
  about being rich, 42
  of immortality, 35
  of self-worth, 109
fees, of professional service providers, 78t, 82, 83–84

"50% Rule, The: Keep More Profits in Your Wallet" (Lucas), 86
financial advisors, 79n. *See also* advisors
financial education
  opportunities for, in wealth management, 79–80, 82
  for wealthy kids from parents, 109, 112–13
financial security, sense of, 1, 11, 25, 48, 57, 64
financial service firms, 77, 79, 82
fixed costs, 51
fixed management fees, 83, 84
flows in wealth, 47f
  bottom line in, 55
  inflows of, 47–48
  outflows of, 51–55
Franklin, Benjamin, 62, 123
Freeman, Rob, 20

G

Galbraith, John Kenneth, 123
"Gambler, The" (Rogers), 71
game of life, tips for winning, 119
Gandhi, Mahatma, 122
Gates, Bill, 114, 123
general theory of everything (Stevenson), 103, 103f
generation gap
  multigenerational governance model and, 93–94, 93f
  power issues in family wealth and, 103–04
generations in family wealth. *See* multigenerational wealth model
Georgia–Pacific Corporation, 108
Getting to Giving: Fundraising the Entrepreneurial Way (Stevenson with Spence), 29–30, 126
gifts
  to charity, 60, 61, 66, 113
  net worth and, 60–61
  as wealth outflow, 54–55
Gladwell, Malcolm, 100
Gleick, James, 23

goals
  financial planning for, 62, 63
  helping children with setting, 57
  Howard's personal life goals, 21, 25, 63–64
  income choices and, 48, 50, 61, 62
  of SFILP, 73
  success and, 117
  trusts and, 60
  wealth management and, 56, 58–59, 80
  working with professionals and, 81, 81*t*
Godfrey, Joline, 112–13
gold, as asset, 46
Goldwyn, Sam, 37
governance
  family meetings for, 100–01
  five-step process in, 100
  philanthropy and, 100
  professional help with, 78*t*, 82, 99
  top-down model of, 89, 98–101
Grant's Interest Rate Observer, 44
Greenleaf, Robin, 105
growth stocks, 42–43

H
happiness, as success dimension, 116, 117*f*
Hart, Myra, 28
Harvard Business Review, 23, 117
Harvard Business School (HBS)
  case method at, 15–16, 19, 22
  friends and colleagues from, 19
  Howard's graduate study at, 15–16
  Howard's teaching and administration career of, 16, 18–19, 20–22, 24, 26, 27–28, 27*i*, 29, 32, 35, 38–39, 68, 121
Harvard Union, 45
Harvard University, 45
Health Care & Retirement Corporation of America, 68
healthy attitudes toward wealth, 109, 110–11
hedge fund managers, 81, 83
Hefner, Hugh, 114

help in investing. *See also* professional help
  personal and informal advice in, 76
helplessness, 34–35
Higginbotham, Grandfather, 8, 9, 10
Higginbotham, Grandmother, 9, 10–11
Higginbotham family, 5–7, 9, 10, 54
Hillel, 115
Holladay, Utah, 9, 10, 11, 12, 13, 15, 16, 63, 67
Holmes, Oliver Wendell, 37
house rules (one of Howard's six truths), 33, 39
Howardopoly, 119, 120*f*
Howard's Gift: Uncommon Wisdom to Inspire Your Life's Work (Sinoway with Meadow), 30, 50, 59, 115
Howard's Journey: Lessons from the Game of Life (Stevenson with Spence), 2, 119

I
IBM, 15
income, 122
  business, 48–49
  choosing right course for, 50–51
  comparing yourself to others on, 62
  definition of wealth involving, 41
  earned, 48
  investment, 49
  measuring wealth using, 60–61
  net, 60
  as wealth inflow, 47, 48–51
income taxes, 53, 55, 66
inflows of wealth, 47*f*, 47–48, 51
inheritance
  deciding on amount of, 114
  multigenerational wealth and, 89–95
  successfully passing to children, 109, 114
  when to distribute money in, 114
  work ethic of children and amount of, 112
inheritance boom, 1
inheritance income, as wealth inflow, 47, 51

investing, 67–75
    betting analogy and, 38, 70, 72, 73, 74, 84
    diversification and, 46, 70, 72, 73
    growth stocks and, 42–43
    Howard's education in, 68–70
    Howard's personal experiences with, 20, 25, 26, 49, 64, 66
    Howard's perspective (principles) on, 71–74
    long-term thinking in, 62, 73
    rightsizing rule in, 74
    rules in, 39
    SFILP case study of, 73–75
    statistical approach to, 70
    sustaining stocks and, 43
    as wealth outflow, 53
investment advisors, 77, 79
investment banking, 16, 20
investment income, 49
investment managers, 78t, 81
investments, types of, in SFILP, 73

J

James, Tom, 68
Just Enough: Tools for Creating Success in Your Work and Life (Nash and Stevenson), 27, 28, 116, 117

K

Kalidasa, 121
Kao, John, 22
Klarman, Seth, 24–25, 69, 70
knowledge, or what you need to know (one of Howard's six truths), 33, 36–37

L

Lack, Simon, 70
lawyers, and wealth management, 60, 77, 78t, 81, 99
leadership, and family wealth, 105–106
Learning by Giving Foundation, 113
legacy, as success dimension, 116, 117f
Lennon, John, 63
leverage, 19, 24, 48, 49, 53, 61, 68
leveraged buyouts (LBOs), 68
leveraged recaps, 69

Lewis, Michael, 70
life insurance, 18, 59, 64, 82
life insurers, 77, 78t
lifetime
    personal changes over, 8, 117
    three periods of, 35–36
Light, Jay, 4, 27i
Liles, Patrick, 58
Lincoln, Abraham, 2, 109-10
Little, Miss (teacher), 13
Little, Royal, 20
"live life forward" philosophy, 13
love, money as expression of, 111
Lucas, Stuart E., 79, 86

M

Mace, Myles, 16
magazines, on wealth management, 79
management theory, 23
margin, 60
"Markets Explained" (Adams), 70
Markowitz, Harry, 70
McArthur, John, 21–22
McCracken, Robert J., 122
Medicare, 1, 51
Memoirs of a Handcart Pioneer (Dee), 8
Mencken, H. L., 122
metrics (scorecards)
    Howard's example of, 65–66, 65f
    wealth management using, 55, 56, 60–61, 119
millionaire households, number of, 1
Mohammed, 122
Moldoveanu, Mihnea, 23
money
    as asset, 45
    emotional meaning of, 40
    healthy attitudes of kids toward, 109, 110–11
money managers, 70, 81, 82–84
Mormon Church, 9
    Howard's childhood and, 12
    personal accountability and, 12, 34
    Stevenson family background and, 5, 8
    values of family, community, and continuous learning in, 12

multifamily offices, 78t, 81, 82
multigenerational wealth model,
    89–95, 92t
  dilemma of passing down wealth in,
    93
  fifth generation family example in,
    92–93, 92t
  generation gap in, 93–94, 93f
  number and dispersal of descendants
    in, 89–92, 90f
  Stevenson family trust example in,
    94–95, 94t

N

Nash, Laura, 27, 116
need assessment, for working with
    professionals, 80–81, 81t
net income, 60
net worth, 60–61, 64, 65
Newton-John, Olivia, 105
Northern Trust, 80

O

O'Brien, Andy, 28
Oliver, Mary, 63n
opportunistic investments, 73
opportunity costs, 44
opportunity investments, 73
outflows of wealth, 47, 47f, 51–55
outsourced CIOs, 78t

P

parents
  challenges in raising kids for,
    109–15
  healthy attitudes about money and,
    109, 110–11
  financial education provided by,
    109, 112–13
  as positive role models, 109, 114–15
  self-esteem in kids and, 109–10
  successfully passing wealth to kids
    by, 109, 114
  work ethic in kids and, 109,
    111–12
performance fees, 24, 84
philanthropy. See also charitable
    giving

family governance and, 100
Howard's involvement in, 20, 22,
    29, 54
wealthy kids and learning about,
    113
as wealth outflow, 54
plans and planning
  in business, 28
  change and, 63
  within families, 99, 109, 110, 116
  in investing, 38
  professional help in, 76, 81–84
  realistic approach to, 63
  in wealth management, 56, 62–63,
    64, 66
Plato, 122
Plautus, 122
Poorvu, Bill, 19–20, 23, 29, 68–69
Popper, Karl, 37
power issues, and family wealth,
    103–04
"Power of Predictability, The"
    (Stevenson and Moldoveanu), 23
Preco, 20, 21
predictability, interest in, 22, 23, 33, 37
predictions
  entrepreneurs and, 23
  as guesses about the future (one
    of Howard's six truths), 33, 34,
    37–38
  investment decisions and, 23, 68, 75
principles
  of family wealth, 102
  of investing, 72
  of wealth management, 56
private equity managers, 81, 83
Private Wealth Management (PWM)
    program, Booth School of
    Business, University of Chicago,
    79
professional help, 76, 81–87
  assessing needs and wants before
    working with, 80–81, 81t
  broad categories of, 81–84
  buyer beware caution in selecting,
    86–87
  market categories served by, 7
    7, 77t

professional help (cont'd)
  need for personal financial education for working with, 79–80
  overview of industry in, 77–79
  people factor in selecting, 84–85
  questions for selecting, 80–86
  respect for and skepticism of, 76
  types of service providers in, 77–79, 78*t*, 79n
  working successfully with, 85–86
proverbs, 104, 123
punishment, in family wealth control, 104

Q

quotations on wealth, 122–23

R

Raising Financially Fit Kids (Godfrey), 112–13
real estate
  Howard's investment in family houses, 17, 19, 20, 24, 28, 52, 53
  Howard's investment in, 20, 22, 64, 68
  as sustaining investment, 43
real estate courses, at HBS, 19–20, 22, 39, 68
real estate investment trusts (REITs), 19, 20
Realty Income Trust, 20
registered investment advisors (RIAs), 77
responsibility
  family, 97, 98
  fiduciary, of wealth managers, 82
  financial, 64, 66, 76, 112
  personal actions and, 34, 63, 99
  teaching children about, 109–10, 112–13
  wealth as, 56, 57–58, 106
retirement
  financial security for, 57
  keys to, 29
  trusts and, 60
rightsizing in investing, 72, 74
Rock, Arthur, 22
Rogers, Kenny, 71

Rogerson, Tom, 59, 98, 99–100, 100n, 105, 109–10, 115
role models, parents as, 109, 114–15
rules
  for family trusts, 97, 99
  in game of life, 119
  for investing (Howard's principles), 72
  in investment decisions, 81, 84, 86
  learning about and deciding to play (one of Howard's six truths), 33, 39
  for rightsizing, 74
  within SFILP, 106
Rural Land Foundation (RLF), 20
Russian proverb, 123

S

Sahlman, Bill, 20n, 22, 68n
salaries, and personal wealth, 48
"Salutation to the Dawn" (Kalidasa), 121
Sarofim, Fayez, 22
saving
  planning for, 62
  as wealth outflow, 53
  wealthy kids and, 112
Scientific Systems Services, 20
scorecards
  Howard's example of, 65–66, 65*f*
  wealth management using, 55, 56, 60–61, 119
self-awareness, of wealthy kids, 110
self-esteem, of wealthy kids, 109–10
Seneca, Lucius Annaeus, 122
service providers. *See* professional help
SFILP. *See* Stevenson Family Investment Limited Partnership
servant leadership, 102, 105
Shakespeare, William, 35
Siegel, Cary, 112n
significance, as success dimension, 116, 117*f*
Silver, Nate, 70
Simmons, Matt, 19, 68
Simmons Associates, 19, 20, 68

six truths (Stevenson), 33–39
　background to, 33–34
　summary of, 33
　wealth management principles
　　related to, 56
Social Security, 1, 51
social welfare as wealth inflow, 47, 51
Socrates, 122
Soffe, Nimrod George, 90f, 91
Sons and Daughters of the American Revolution, 8
spectrum, wealth as, 44–45, 44f
Spence, Shirley, 2, 28, 29, 31
spending
　planning for, 62
　by wealthy kids, 112
　as wealth outflow, 51–52
Stanford University, 13–15, 15i, 17, 111
statistical models, in investing, 70
stepchildren, 25, 97
Stevenson, Andy (son), 20, 24, 25, 28, 29, 52, 53, 55, 60, 75, 76, 81, 106, 112, 114
Stevenson, Charley (son), 19, 25, 28, 52, 53, 55, 76, 112, 114
Stevenson, Craig (brother), 9, 10, 12–13, 15, 94, 95, 97–98, 106
Stevenson, Dorothy Higginbotham (mother), 8, 9–10, 11, 13, 18, 26, 94, 106, 118
Stevenson, Fredi (wife), 25–26, 29, 30–31, 61, 64, 100, 102, 113
Stevenson, Grandfather, 8, 11, 12
Stevenson, Howard, 4–32
　ancestral charts of, 5, 6i–7i, 90f, 91
　board memberships of, 20, 25, 29, 31, 43, 53, 64, 68, 70
　books by, 2, 23, 29–30, 127
　career decisions of, 14–16, 17, 19, 20, 21
　career review for, 18–29
　childhood years of, 9–13, 9i, 11i, 24, 111
　children and family life of, 18, 19, 19i, 21, 24, 25, 26, 30–31, 30i, 36, 102, 111
　chronological review of life journey of, 4–32
　college education of, 13–15, 15i
　definition of wealth of, 42–46
　early jobs of, in aunt and uncle's business, 11, 14
　family book (*Howard's Journey*) by, 2, 119
　family wealth philosophy of, 102–07
　father's and mother's values and, 10, 11
　general theory of everything of, 103, 103f
　HBS graduate school experience of, 15–16
　HBS teaching and administration career of, 16, 18–19, 20–22, 24, 26, 27–28, 27i, 29, 32, 35, 38–39, 68, 121
　heart attack of, 28, 31, 36
　heritage of, 5–9, 106–07
　higher education of, 13–17
　houses and house projects of, 17, 19, 20, 24, 28, 52, 53
　influences of community, family, and teachers on, 13
　investing education of, 68–70
　investing perspective (principles) of, 71–74
　investment decisions of, 20, 25, 26, 64
　marriages of, 16–17, 25, 30–31, 54
　Mormon background of, 5, 8, 12
　nonprofit work of, 29, 31
　parents of, 9–13, 18
　philanthropy of, 20, 29, 54
　pioneer background of, 8
　reflections on life by, 31–32
　scorecard example of, 65–66, 65f
　six truths of, 33–39, 56
　two-stage strategy for building wealth used by, 64–65
　uncle's influence on, 11–12
　wealth goals of, 63–64
　wealth management principles of, 56–63
Stevenson, Ralph (father), 5, 9–10, 11, 13, 15, 18, 26, 63, 91, 98

Stevenson, Susan (sister), 10, 12–13, 94, 95
Stevenson, Will (son), 18, 19*i*, 24, 25, 28, 52, 53, 55, 76, 112, 113, 114
Stevenson family
    ancestral charts for, 5, 6*i*–7*i*, 90*f*, 91
    Mormon background of, 5, 8, 9
    number and dispersal of multigenerational descendants in, 91
    pioneer background of, 8
    tracing lineage of, 5–7
Stevenson Family Investment Limited Partnership (SFILP)
    analysis of outcomes in, 74, 75
    broad types of investments in, 73, 74
    goal of, 73
    Howard's found of and work with, 26, 28
    investing case study with, 73–75
    partners and leadership in, 105–106, 113
    professional help for, 80–81
    voluntary associations of members in, 105
Sting, 105
success
    attitudes toward wealth and models of, 111
    dimensions of, 116–17, 117*f*
    family celebrations of, 105, 110
    Howard's mother's motto on, 10
    parents' relationship with kids and, 115–16
    revisiting vision and strategies for, over lifetime, 118
    rewards for, 51, 52, 54
    ways to define, 59, 104, 115–16
succession plans, 99
Success That Lasts (Nash and Stevenson), 117
Sudbury Valley Trustees (SVT), 25, 29
sustaining stocks, 42, 43

T
tax accountants, 76, 77, 78*t*
taxes
    business income and, 49
    divorce and, 25
    estate, 55, 64
    family wealth planning and, 92, 92*t*, 111
    income, 53, 55, 66
    investment income and, 49
    mortgages and, 53
    professional assistant with, 76, 78*t*, 80, 82, 86
    trusts and, 60
Thoreau, Henry, 58, 123
three-legged approach to wealth management, 59–60
TONE (Timber Owners of New England), 43
top-down family governance, 89, 98–101
total wealth, 60, 61, 65
track records, in selecting service providers, 85
traditional investment management firms, 81, 83
transaction costs, 44
transparency, in selecting service providers, 85
trustees, 20, 59, 60, 76
trusts
    charitable, 26, 53, 54, 66, 100
    deciding on amount of, 114
    divorce and, 25, 60, 92
    goals and, 59–60
    governance issues in, 99
    Stevenson family trust example of, 94–95, 94*t*, 98
    types of, 60
    when to distribute money in, 114
2 + 20 formula, in money management, 83

U
University of Chicago, Booth School of Business, 79

Utah, Stevenson family background in, 8, 10, 12, 13, 24, 63, 67, 91, 106–07

V
vacations, family, 112
values
   from family and community, 13
   of Howard's parents, 10, 11
   "live life forward" philosophy in, 13
   Mormon, of family, community, and continuous learning, 12
   parents as role models for, 114
variable costs, 51

W
Walden (Thoreau), 58
Wales, Stevenson family roots in, 5
WCVB-TV, 69
wealth, 41–55
   bottom line in, 47f, 55
   comparing yourself to others on, 62
   decisions about how much money needed and, 61–62
   dynamics of, 46–47
   emotional meaning of money and, 40
   families and. *See* family wealth
   flywheel metaphor for, 47
   as gift and not right, 110
   goals needed for, 58–59
   healthy attitudes of kids toward, 109, 110–11
   Howard's definition of, 42–46
   Howard's goals for, 63–64
   Howard's two-stage strategy for building, 64–65
   inflows in, 47f, 47–48, 51
   as instrument of choice, 57–58
   as instrument of control, 57, 103–04
   nature and dynamics of, 41–55
   outflows in, 47f, 51–55
   quotations on, 122–23
   raising children in context of, 2
   range of personal meanings of, 41, 122–23
   as responsibility, 56, 57–58, 106
   as spectrum, 44–45, 44f
   stages of needs and wants in, 61–61
   traditional definitions of, 41–42
wealth advisors, 81, 82, 85
Wealth: Grow It and Protect It (Lucas), 79
wealth management, 56–66
   assessing needs and wants in, 80–81, 81t
   case study on, 63–66
   diversification and, 46, 70, 72, 73
   goals needed for, 58–59
   Howard's principles on, 56–63
   Howard's two-stage strategy for building wealth and, 64–65
   need for personal financial education for, 79–80
   planning in, 62–63
   professional help in, 76–87
   scorecards for monitoring, 60–61
   service providers in. *See* professional help
   three-legged approach to, 59–60
wealth management industry, 77–79
   buyer beware caution in working with, 86–87
   market categories served by, 77, 77t
   need for personal financial education for working with, 79–80
   overview of industry, 77–79
   questions for selecting providers in, 80–86
   respect for and skepticism of, 76
   service providers in, 77–79, 78t, 79n
   size of, 77
   types of service providers in, 77–79, 78t, 79n
wealth managers, 81, 82
wealthy kids, 2, 108–18
   challenges for wealthy parents raising, 109–15
   childhood chores and jobs for, 112
   differences between the older and younger generations' circumstances and perspectives in, 108–09
   family vacations and, 112
   financial education for working with, 80

wealthy kids (cont'd)
   financial responsibility to, 57
   healthy attitudes about money in, 109, 110–11
   parents as positive role models for, 109, 114–15
   philanthropy and, 113
   self-esteem of, 109–10
   successfully passing wealth from parents to, 109, 114
   teachings and learnings summarized by, 116
   work ethic in, 109, 111–12
Weil, Simone, 123
Wharton School of Business, Wealth Management Initiative, 79–80
Wealth Management Unwrapped (Beyer), 79
wealth professionals, 1, 3, 89, 99. *See also* professional help
   getting help from, 76–87
Wealth Strategist Partners, 79
wealth transfer, and inheritance boom, 1

Webster's Dictionary, 41
Wharton School of Business, 79–80
"Wheeler Dealers, The" (film), 16
Whittier, John Greenleaf, 118
Why Didn't They Teach Me This in School? 99 Personal Money Management Principles to Live By (Siegel), 112
Wikipedia, 41, 42
Wilde, Peter, 20
Williams Group, 98
Wolfe, Fritz, 68
Wolfe Industries, 20, 68
work ethic, 109, 111–12
World War II, 9–10
Wyss, HansJoerg, 27i, 29
Wyss Institute for Biologically Inspired Engineering, 29

Y

Yogananda, 122

Z

Zimbabwe dollar, 45, 45f

PRAISE FOR *WEALTH AND FAMILIES*

Howard Stevenson is a wise man. This personal narrative marries decades of real life experience with an academic's unbiased search for the truth. Enjoy his pithy, pointed writing style and you will be rewarded with new insights on wealth and families and a fun read.

Stuart Lucas, Chairman of Wealth Strategist Partners, a fourth-generation heir of the founder of the Carnation Company, and author of *Wealth: Grow It and Protect It*

Wealth is what happens when you reach financial escape velocity—when your money works while you sleep. Wealth is very hard to create and really easy to destroy. And, it can be destructive for individuals and families. Howard has written a terrific book, full of wisdom and wit, that serves as a helpful guide for creating, sustaining, and sharing wealth in a positive, purposeful way.

William A. Sahlman, Harvard Business School Professor and Senior Associate Dean of External Relations

Wealth and Families *is the best book about the subject that I have read in a long time. Howard Stevenson's wisdom about wealth is informed by experience and infused with humility. In the end,* Wealth and Families *isn't so much a book about getting and staying rich (though it will certainly help readers do that). It's a book about living a good and rewarding life.*

Richard Bradley, Editor-in-Chief, *Worth*

From a small town in Utah to becoming a professor at HBS to co-founding Baupost, one of the nation's best performing hedge funds, Stevenson shares his perspectives on investing, wealth and—most importantly—the notion of success. Wealth and Families *contains many insightful, often contrarian, observations about how best to manage your wealth and not ruin your family.*

Spencer B. Burke, Executive at The St. Louis Trust Company, a multifamily office

PRAISE FOR *WEALTH AND FAMILIES* (Cont'd)

I greatly enjoyed this book—speed reading it first and then returning to thought-provoking chapters about how to build, manage, and pass on wealth. Extrapolating from Stevenson's personal journey to the broader topics of wealth and families makes it especially interesting and powerful.

Howard Cox, former General Partner of
Greylock and former Chairman of the
National Venture Capital Association

Reading Wealth and Families *is like having a good talk with a friend about subjects near and dear to your heart. I am giving a copy to each of my children!*

Michael O'Connell, Senior Managing Director
of M20, a family investment office

Wealth and Families *is a modern "The Gospel of Wealth." From a leading business educator who has helped many students learn how to fail their way to success comes a candid, personal, comprehensive story about how to avoid succeeding one's way to failure ... great lessons on the challenging task of being a steward of substantial wealth.*

John E. Abele, Founding Chairman, Retired,
Boston Scientific Corporation

Howard Stevenson has always been a great thinker, brimming with new ideas and fresh perspectives. I can't think of anyone who wouldn't benefit from a dose of Howard's accumulated lifetime of wisdom and insight.

Seth A. Klarman, President and CEO,
Baupost Group LLC

The discussion of issues around money and one's children is tempting for too many of us to delay, defer, and delay again. Howard's wise book will prod and catalyze that tough but essential discussion. He has a remarkable talent for teaching without being preachy.

James M. Stone, Founder, Chairman, and
CEO of Plymouth Rock Assurance

PRAISE FOR *WEALTH AND FAMILIES* (Cont'd)

Stevenson's book, Wealth and Families: Lessons from My Life Journey, *is a "how to do it" book. Essentially, it describes how he did it, weaving together his experiences in different but related areas such as teaching, investing, and philanthropy. It should be part of anyone's "entrepreneurial studies." Plus it is fun to read!*

C. D. Spangler, Jr., President Emeritus,
University of North Carolina

This unique and exceptional memoir is a tutorial on family capital—both financial and human. Rich with juicy, instructive stories, it will hold the interest of any family member. Elder generations will nod in recognition at some of the truths that Stevenson shares, millennials will find a road map for navigating the choices of becoming . . . and I intend to share whole portions of the book with every teenager I know.

Joline Godfrey, author of *Raising Financially Fit Kids* and founder of Independent Means, a financial education services provider

I always tell business school students that their goal should be to lead a rich life, not make a lot of money. Howard Stevenson has been generous to share his wisdom and experiences in his latest publication. While this book has valuable insights into investing and accumulating wealth, it will help you achieve the more important goal of living and sustaining a balanced, rewarding life.

David Abrams, Managing Partner of
Abrams Capital Management

Howard Stevenson has managed to do something no one has managed to do before: produce a life manual for families with even a moderate level of wealth. Wealth and Families *illustrates that building and managing a family network is a multidimensional journey—a journey that never ends—with each decision defining future options in areas from finances to family relations. It is a must read for any family with assets.*

Daniel Muzyka, President and CEO of the Conference Board of Canada, RBC Financial Group Professor of Entrepreneurship, University of British Columbia

PRAISE FOR *WEALTH AND FAMILIES*
(Cont'd)

It's hard to fathom—even once you've read it—the compactness of the wisdom and insight Howard Stevenson provides in this short book. His perspective is practical, yet enormously synthetic. Don't be confused by the direct, "awe-shucks" tone.

The simple folksy-sounding analysis of the complex problem of intergenerational wealth belies Howard's incorporation and absorption of much more than the magic of mathematically rigorous laws of compounding and diversification, sprinkling in a foundational knowledge of the tax code and the law. It's that he has, in his own mental frame, incorporated a sense of people's humanity, their strengths and weaknesses, their goals and actual accomplishments, based on successfully watching, and doing, for all these years.

The wisest teachers have all along been life's best and most observant students. Howard—and this integrative little book that you and your progeny should share—are just that.

Kenneth A. Froot, Harvard Business School
Professor Emeritus

HOW TO ORDER AND CUSTOMIZE
WEALTH AND FAMILIES

Individual Purchases

Wealth and Families is available through amazon.com in paperback, hard cover and kindle formats.

Volume Purchases

Special discounts (10-40%) are available on purchases of over 50 copies of *Wealth and Families*.

Customized Editions

For institutions interested in distributing more than 200 copies to your constituents, we can customize the cover (e.g., add "Compliments of" and your name and logo) and add a page of text (e.g., information about your services) for an additional fee.

For Volume Purchases and Customization

Please visit our website at *www.wealthandfamilies.com* or contact the publisher:

        Timberline LLC
        P.O. Box 639
        Belmont, MA 02478

        Email: *wealthandfamilies@gmail.com*

www.ingramcontent.com/pod-product-compliance
Lightning Source LLC
Chambersburg PA
CBHW040723240426

43666CB00045B/2907